Financial Decisions

How to Reduce Mistakes, Limit Risk, and Make Better Decisions Under Uncertainty

Mark Ellison

PERENNIAL PUBLISHING

Published by Perennial Publishing

First Edition

Paperback ISBN: 978-1-971996-30-1
Hardcover ISBN: 978-1-971996-31-8
EBook ISBN: 978-1-971996-32-5

For bulk or institutional orders, contact Perennial Publishing.

Contents

Decisions as Structural Events

Decisions are commonly interpreted as discrete moments—points at which a choice is made and an outcome follows. Within a financial system, this framing is incomplete. A decision is not a contained event. It is a directional shift within an existing structure. The system does not pause, receive a decision, and then resume. It is already in motion, already carrying constraints, exposures, and prior configurations forward. The decision interacts with that motion. It alters direction, not by replacing the system's trajectory, but by bending it.

A trajectory is not defined by a single point. It is defined by the sequence of points and the direction they collectively establish. When a decision occurs, it does not exist in isolation from prior decisions or future ones. It is embedded within a sequence. The effect of the decision is therefore not limited to its immediate outcome. Its primary effect is the change it introduces to the path the system is already following. This change may be subtle or pronounced, but it is cumulative. The system continues forward along a modified path, carrying the consequences of that directional adjustment into subsequent states.

Single-event thinking isolates the moment of decision and evaluates it independently. It assigns importance based on perceived magnitude, visibility, or immediate consequence. Under this framing, certain decisions are labeled significant while others are treated as negligible. Within a system, this distinction is unstable. The significance of a decision is not determined by how it appears at the moment it is made. It is determined by how it interacts with the system's structure and where it occurs along the trajectory. A decision that appears minor may occur at a point of structural sensitivity, where small directional changes produce large downstream divergence. A decision that appears major may occur in a region of structural stability, where its effect is absorbed and dissipated without altering the long-term path.

Sequencing governs how decisions accumulate. Each decision is made within the context created by previous decisions, and it sets the conditions for those that follow. This creates path dependency. The system's future states are not only influenced by current decisions, but constrained by the sequence that led to them. Once a trajectory is established, subsequent decisions operate within a narrower range of feasible directions. Options are not evaluated in an abstract space; they are evaluated within the boundaries defined by prior structure. The system's history is not informational—it is structural. It determines what the system can absorb, what it can sustain, and how it responds to further directional changes.

Directional drift emerges from this accumulation. It is not the result of a single large deviation, but the compounded effect of multiple smaller shifts. Each decision adjusts the trajectory incrementally. Over time, these adjustments produce divergence between the original path and the current one. The system may appear stable in the short term because each individual shift is within tolerance. However, the cumulative effect can reposition the system into a different structural region, where its capacity to absorb disturbance is altered. Drift is therefore not visible through isolated evaluation. It becomes visible only when the sequence is considered as a continuous trajectory.

The position of a decision within the system determines its impact. Position is defined by the system's current configuration—its exposure levels, its constraints, its available capacity, and its proximity to structural thresholds. A decision made when the system is distant from constraint behaves differently from one made when the system is near a limit.

The same directional adjustment can be absorbed in one context and destabilizing in another. Impact is therefore conditional. It is not inherent to the decision itself, but emerges from the interaction between the decision and the system's state at the moment of application.

This reframing removes the notion of isolated importance. Decisions do not carry fixed weight. Their influence is relational and context-dependent. The system does not categorize decisions as large or small; it responds to how each decision alters trajectory within the current structural configuration. Evaluation based on perceived significance obscures this relationship. It directs attention toward visible events rather than underlying direction. The system, however, evolves through direction, not visibility.

The structure through which decisions are made can be separated from the outcomes that follow. Process refers to this structure. It encompasses the rules, constraints, and mechanisms that govern how decisions are generated and applied. It defines the conditions under which decisions are made, including the information available, the time allowed, and the tolerances within which the system operates. Outcomes are the observable results that occur after decisions interact with the system. They are expressions of system behavior at specific points in time.

Outcomes are often used as indicators of decision quality. This inference assumes a direct and reliable link between the decision and the result. Within a system operating under uncertainty, this link is unstable. Outcomes are influenced by variables that are not fully controlled or predictable at the moment of decision. External conditions, timing interactions, and random variation all contribute to the result. A decision made within a stable and coherent process may produce an unfavorable outcome due to external disturbance. Conversely, a decision made within a flawed process may produce a favorable outcome if external conditions temporarily align.

Because of this, outcomes cannot serve as consistent indicators of the underlying process. They provide information about what occurred, but not necessarily about how the system is structured to produce future results. When outcomes are used to evaluate decisions, the evaluation becomes sensitive to variability. Short-term success can reinforce processes that contain structural weaknesses, because the immediate result appears to validate the decision. These weaknesses remain embedded in the system and may not be exposed until conditions change. When they do, the system may experience abrupt instability, not because of a sudden deterioration in decision-making, but because the underlying process was misaligned from the beginning.

Process stability determines how the system behaves across sequences of decisions. A stable process maintains consistent structure under varying conditions. It produces decisions that are aligned with the system's constraints and capacities, regardless of short-term fluctuations in outcome. This does not eliminate variability in results. It ensures that the system remains within a range where variability can be absorbed without structural failure. The focus shifts from evaluating individual outcomes to evaluating whether the process maintains coherence across different states.

Short-term outcomes can mask structural flaws because they represent isolated points along the trajectory. A favorable outcome may occur even if the process is introducing directional drift toward instability. The system may appear to be functioning correctly because no immediate disruption is visible. However, the underlying trajectory may be moving toward a region where the system's tolerance is reduced. When this region is reached, subsequent variability that would have been absorbed earlier may now produce disproportionate impact. The delay between process misalignment and outcome manifestation creates a false sense of stability.

Separating process from outcome allows the system to be evaluated on structural terms. The question becomes whether the process produces decisions that maintain directional coherence and respect system constraints, not whether individual outcomes are favorable. This distinction reduces the influence of variability on evaluation. It anchors assessment in the structure that generates decisions rather than in the results that follow them. The system's long-term behavior is determined by this structure, not by isolated outcomes.

Decision environments are inherently uncertain. At the moment a decision is made, the full set of variables that will influence the outcome is not known. Some variables are observable, others are latent, and many interact in ways that are not fully predictable. This uncertainty is not an occasional disruption. It is a constant condition. The system operates continuously within it. Decisions are therefore made without complete information and without certainty regarding their consequences.

Repetition is the mechanism through which the system's structure is exposed under these conditions. A single decision does not provide sufficient information to evaluate how the system behaves. It is only through repeated decision cycles that patterns emerge. Each cycle introduces variation in conditions. The process is applied repeatedly across these variations, and the system's responses accumulate. Over time, the interaction between process and variability reveals whether the system maintains stability or drifts toward instability.

Repetition amplifies both strengths and weaknesses. A process that is structurally aligned will produce decisions that keep the system within its tolerance range across multiple cycles. Variability will still produce fluctuations in outcomes, but the system will not approach structural thresholds. A process that contains misalignment may produce acceptable results in early cycles, especially if variability is favorable. However, as repetition continues, the cumulative effect of small misalignments becomes more pronounced. The system may gradually move toward a region where its ability to absorb variability is reduced. When variability shifts, the system may experience rapid degradation.

Variability is not an anomaly that can be removed. It is an inherent feature of the environment in which the system operates. Conditions change, interactions shift, and external factors introduce dispersion in outcomes. The system cannot be designed to eliminate variability. It must be structured to function within it. This requires that the decision process remains coherent even when outcomes deviate from expectation. If the process is dependent on stable outcomes to function, it becomes fragile when variability increases.

The absence of outcome certainty means that decisions cannot be evaluated solely on their immediate results. The system must rely on the consistency of the process across repeated cycles. Each decision contributes to the trajectory, and the accumulation of these contributions determines the system's position relative to its constraints. Repetition exposes whether the system is moving toward or away from regions of instability. It reveals whether the process maintains directional alignment under different conditions.

This exposure is gradual. The system does not reveal its structural characteristics in a single instance. It requires multiple iterations, each interacting with varying conditions. The process is tested implicitly through its repeated application. Stability is not declared; it is observed through the system's ability to maintain coherence over time. Instability is not triggered by a single failure; it emerges when repeated decisions move the system into a configuration where it cannot absorb further variation.

The interaction between trajectory, process, and repetition defines how decisions influence system stability. Each decision alters direction within an existing structure. The process determines how these decisions are generated and applied. Repetition exposes how the process performs under uncertainty. These elements are not independent. They operate simultaneously, each influencing the others. The trajectory evolves through repeated application of the process under varying conditions.

Decision quality, within this framework, is not defined by isolated success. It is defined by the structural consistency of the process as it produces decisions across repeated cycles. A high-quality decision process maintains alignment with system constraints and capacities, regardless of short-term variability in outcomes. It produces decisions that adjust trajectory in a way that preserves the system's ability to absorb future variation. A low-quality process introduces misalignment, even if immediate outcomes appear favorable. It shifts the trajectory toward regions where the system's tolerance is reduced.

As decisions accumulate, the effect of the process becomes embedded in the system's structure. The trajectory reflects the cumulative influence of repeated directional adjustments. If these adjustments are consistent with maintaining stability, the system remains within its tolerance range. If they are not, the system gradually approaches structural thresholds. The transition from stability to instability is not marked by a single event. It is the result of accumulated directional shifts that position the system where it can no longer absorb variation.

Stability is therefore not the outcome of isolated successful decisions. It is the result of a process that produces consistent directional alignment over time. The system does not require perfect decisions to remain stable. It requires that the process governing decisions does not introduce cumulative misalignment. Imperfect decisions can be absorbed if the overall trajectory remains within tolerance. Conversely, a sequence of decisions that individually appear acceptable can collectively produce instability if they consistently shift the trajectory in an unfavorable direction.

Decision quality, in structural terms, is the ability of the process to maintain coherence under uncertainty. It is not measured by the absence of unfavorable outcomes, but by the system's capacity to continue functioning without approaching failure. This capacity is determined by how decisions interact with the system's structure over time. The focus shifts from evaluating moments to evaluating mechanisms. Decisions are not isolated acts of choice; they are components of a system that evolves through their repeated application.

Within this perspective, decisions function as mechanisms that translate uncertainty into trajectory. Each decision takes place under incomplete information and contributes to the system's direction. The process through which decisions are made determines how this translation occurs. Repetition reveals whether the translation maintains stability or introduces drift. The system's behavior is the cumulative expression of these interactions. Stability is not imposed through individual actions. It emerges from the structural consistency of decisions applied over time.

The Rationality Illusion Mechanism

Decision-making is often framed as an exercise conducted under ideal conditions. Within that framing, a decision is assumed to emerge from complete information, unrestricted time, and the absence of external pressure. All relevant variables are presumed observable. Alternatives can be evaluated without urgency. The system is assumed to be stable while evaluation occurs. Under these conditions, logic appears sufficient. The decision is treated as the output of a process that is unconstrained by the environment in which it operates.

These conditions do not exist within financial systems. The system is not static at the moment of decision. It continues to move, carrying forward obligations, exposures, and prior configurations. Information is incomplete because not all variables are visible or measurable at the time the decision is required. Time is limited because decisions must be made within intervals defined by external and internal constraints. Pressure is present because the system is already engaged with commitments that cannot be deferred indefinitely. The absence of these ideal conditions is not an occasional deviation. It is the baseline state under which decisions occur.

Constraint therefore becomes the governing condition of decision-making. A constraint is not a secondary influence applied after evaluation. It defines the boundaries within which evaluation can take place. Time constrains how long the system can remain in a state of indecision before consequences begin to accumulate. Information constrains what can be known about the variables influencing the outcome. Capacity constrains the system's ability to process information, consider alternatives, and absorb potential error. Exposure constrains the consequences associated with different directions the system might take. Each of these constraints operates continuously, shaping the decision environment before any logical comparison of options begins.

Time constraint limits the depth of evaluation. The system cannot indefinitely delay a decision without incurring cost or risk. As time compresses, the range of analysis narrows. Information constraint limits the accuracy of evaluation. Unknown variables and incomplete data prevent full modeling of outcomes. Capacity constraint limits the number of variables that can be processed simultaneously. The system cannot integrate all possible interactions within a finite cognitive and structural bandwidth. Exposure constraint limits tolerance for error. When the system is positioned near structural thresholds, the acceptable range of outcomes narrows, reducing the margin within which decisions can vary without causing instability.

These constraints define the decision space. The decision space is not the set of all theoretically possible options. It is the subset of options that can be evaluated and executed within the current constraints. Logic operates inside this space. It does not expand it. Before any comparison of alternatives occurs, the constraints have already determined which alternatives are accessible, which are visible, and which can be acted upon. The structure of the decision is therefore shaped prior to evaluation. Logic does not determine the boundaries of the decision. It operates within boundaries already imposed by the system.

Financial systems operate within continuous motion. Income arrives and fluctuates, expenses are incurred, obligations persist, and external conditions change. The system does not isolate decision points from this motion. A decision is made while the system is already engaged in multiple processes. These processes do not pause to allow for evaluation. They continue to evolve, altering the conditions under which the decision is being made. The system's state at the beginning of evaluation is not the same as its state at the moment of execution. This temporal shift introduces additional variability into the decision environment.

The operating environment is defined by overlapping pressures. Timing pressure arises from the sequencing of inflows and outflows, where the alignment between them is imperfect. Obligations impose fixed or semi-fixed demands on the system that must be met regardless of other conditions. Uncertainty introduces variability in both inflows and outflows, as well as in external factors that influence system behavior. These pressures do not act independently. They interact, creating compounded constraint. A timing mismatch may increase exposure, which in turn reduces capacity to absorb further variability. The interaction of pressures produces a dynamic environment in which the system must operate.

Within this environment, constraints do not remain static. Time constraint can tighten as deadlines approach. Information constraint can shift as new data becomes available or as uncertainty increases. Capacity constraint can fluctuate based on system load and prior commitments. Exposure constraint can expand or contract depending on the system's current position relative to its thresholds. Decisions are therefore made within a moving boundary. The decision space itself changes during the evaluation process. This movement further limits the ability to conduct comprehensive analysis.

Competing constraints interact in ways that prevent full optimization. Increasing the depth of evaluation requires time, which may not be available without increasing exposure. Seeking additional information may delay action, which may not be feasible given existing obligations. Expanding the range of considered alternatives requires capacity, which may already be allocated to managing current system demands. Each constraint cannot be relaxed independently without affecting others. The system must operate within a configuration where constraints are interdependent.

The result is that decisions are made within compressed and imperfect conditions. Compression refers to the reduction in available time, information, and capacity relative to what would be required for ideal evaluation. Imperfection refers to the inability to fully model or predict outcomes due to incomplete information and environmental variability. These conditions are not temporary disruptions. They define the operational baseline. The system is continuously making decisions under compression and imperfection.

Evaluation depth is limited by this environment. Depth refers to the extent to which alternatives can be analyzed, compared, and modeled. Under ideal conditions, depth could be extended until all relevant variables are considered. Under constraint, depth is truncated. The system must select from a limited set of evaluated options, often without fully understanding their long-term implications. The decision is therefore not the result of exhaustive analysis, but of constrained evaluation within a limited window.

The assumption of rational decision-making is built on the premise that decisions are made under ideal conditions. Rationality, in this context, implies that the decision-maker has access to complete information, sufficient time to evaluate all alternatives, and the capacity to process this information without distortion. Under these conditions, the decision that maximizes expected outcome can be identified and selected. This model treats the decision as a function of logic applied to a fully defined set of variables.

This assumption misrepresents how decisions occur within financial systems. Because constraints define the decision space, the set of alternatives considered is incomplete. Because time is limited, evaluation is truncated. Because information is partial, the model of the environment is approximate. Logic is still applied, but it is applied within these limitations. The output of this process is not the optimal decision under ideal conditions. It is the decision that emerges from applying logic within a constrained and evolving environment.

Logic does not operate independently of constraint. It is shaped by what can be known, how much time is available, and how much capacity can be allocated to evaluation. When information is incomplete, logic must operate on assumptions or estimates. When time is limited, logic must prioritize certain variables over others. When capacity is constrained, logic cannot integrate all interactions within the system. The structure of the reasoning process is therefore influenced by the constraints that define the decision environment.

Limited information alters evaluation by introducing uncertainty into the variables being considered. The system cannot fully assess the probability or magnitude of outcomes because not all influencing factors are observable. This leads to decisions being based on partial representations of the system. Time limitation alters evaluation by forcing prioritization. Certain aspects of the decision are analyzed while others are excluded due to lack of time. Capacity limitation alters evaluation by restricting the complexity of the models that can be used. The system cannot simultaneously account for all interactions and dependencies.

Perceived rationality often emerges as a post-hoc interpretation. After an outcome is observed, the decision is reconstructed as if it were made under a coherent and comprehensive evaluation process. The constraints present at the time of decision are not fully represented in this reconstruction. The decision is evaluated against the outcome, and if the outcome is favorable, the decision is labeled rational. If the outcome is unfavorable, the decision is labeled flawed. This interpretation assumes that the decision could have been made differently under the same conditions, without fully accounting for the constraints that shaped it.

This creates a disconnect between how decisions are experienced within the system and how they are evaluated after the fact. Within the system, decisions are bounded by constraints and made under uncertainty. In evaluation, these constraints are often abstracted away, and the decision is assessed as if it were made under ideal conditions. The evaluation therefore does not reflect the structure of the decision environment. It reflects an idealized model that does not exist in operation.

Decisions are structurally bounded. Their form is determined by the constraints that define the decision space, the environment in which they occur, and the limited capacity available for evaluation. Logic operates within these bounds, but does not remove them. The outcome of the decision is therefore not solely a function of logical reasoning. It is the result of reasoning applied within a constrained system. The rationality attributed to the decision is conditional on these constraints, not independent of them.

When decisions are treated as fully rational outputs, the structural conditions under which they are made are obscured. The system is assumed to be capable of producing optimal decisions given sufficient effort or analysis. This assumption introduces blind spots. It directs attention toward improving evaluation without addressing the constraints that shape the decision space. It assumes that better outcomes can be achieved by refining logic, without considering whether the environment allows for such refinement.

Misframing begins at this point. When decisions are interpreted as if they occur under ideal conditions, the role of constraint is minimized or ignored. The system is evaluated based on an assumption that does not match its operating conditions. This leads to incorrect conclusions about decision quality. A decision made under severe constraint may be evaluated as poor because the outcome is unfavorable, without recognizing that the available alternatives were limited. A decision made under favorable conditions may be evaluated as high quality because the outcome is positive, even if the process was structurally weak.

This misframing affects how the system is understood. It suggests that instability arises from incorrect choices rather than from the conditions under which those choices are made. It implies that improving decision outcomes requires better selection among alternatives, rather than examining how the decision space is defined by constraints. The focus shifts toward the surface of decision-making, rather than the structure that governs it.

Structural failure begins with this misinterpretation. When the role of constraint is not accounted for, the system's vulnerabilities remain unaddressed. The decision process may appear adequate under certain conditions, but its limitations are not visible until the system is exposed to increased pressure or variability. When constraints tighten, the inadequacies of the process become apparent, often abruptly. The system may not have the capacity to adapt because the underlying structure was never aligned with the conditions under which decisions are actually made.

Understanding decisions as constrained system mechanisms changes the frame of analysis. It shifts attention from evaluating isolated decisions to examining the structure that produces them. It recognizes that decisions are not free-form outputs of logic, but responses generated within a bounded environment. The system's stability depends not on the elimination of constraint, which is not possible, but on how the decision process operates within it.

Constraint, environment, and the limits of rational evaluation are not separate considerations. They are integrated components of the mechanism through which decisions function. The system does not alternate between ideal and constrained states. It operates continuously under constraint. Decisions emerge from this condition, shaped by it at every stage. The perception of rationality arises from an abstract model that does not account for these conditions. When this perception is applied to evaluate real decisions, it creates a gap between how the system operates and how it is understood.

This gap defines the Rationality Illusion Mechanism. It is not an error in logic, but an error in framing. It assumes that decisions can be evaluated independently of the constraints that define them. It treats outcomes as reflections of decision quality without fully accounting for the environment in which those decisions were made. As a result, it obscures the structural factors that determine system behavior. Decisions are interpreted as isolated moments of choice, rather than as components of a constrained and evolving system.

Recognizing this mechanism requires reorienting the analysis of decisions toward the conditions under which they occur. It requires acknowledging that constraint defines the decision space, that the environment limits evaluation, and that rationality operates within these bounds rather than outside them. When decisions are understood in this way, their role within the system becomes clearer. They are not idealized selections among fully known alternatives. They are structural responses generated under limitation, contributing to the system's trajectory over time.

The Decision Pressure Mechanism

Pressure enters a financial system as a modification of the conditions under which decisions are made. It does not change the necessity of decision-making, but it alters the structure of the decision environment. Under pressure, the system does not gain additional resources to evaluate choices. It operates with reduced time, constrained capacity, and shifting exposure. The result is not simply faster decision-making. It is a different form of decision-making, produced under compressed conditions that reshape how evaluation occurs.

Time pressure is the most immediate form of this compression. It reduces the window within which a decision must be made. The system is no longer able to extend evaluation until sufficient clarity is reached. Instead, it must act within a shortened interval, often defined by external deadlines or internal sequencing requirements. This compression changes the nature of evaluation. The system cannot examine all variables or model all possible outcomes. It must select a subset of information and proceed.

Reduced time directly limits evaluation depth. Depth requires the ability to explore interactions between variables, assess contingencies, and consider multiple pathways. When time is compressed, these layers cannot be fully developed. The system shifts from layered analysis to surface-level assessment. It prioritizes immediacy over completeness. This does not occur as a deliberate preference. It is a structural consequence of insufficient time relative to the complexity of the decision.

Sequencing is disrupted under these conditions. In an unconstrained environment, decisions can be ordered in a way that allows earlier choices to inform later ones. Time pressure collapses this sequence. Decisions that would normally occur in a staged manner are forced into closer proximity or simultaneous execution. The system loses the ability to incorporate feedback between steps. This increases the likelihood that later decisions are made without the informational benefit of earlier outcomes, creating discontinuity in the decision chain.

Time pressure also forces shifts in prioritization. When the system cannot address all decision requirements within the available window, it must allocate attention unevenly. Certain elements are addressed, while others are deferred or excluded. This allocation is not necessarily aligned with structural importance. It is often aligned with immediacy—what must be resolved within the compressed interval. As a result, the system's attention is redistributed based on time sensitivity rather than long-term impact.

Under time pressure, decisions become structurally simplified. Simplification does not imply reduced significance. It refers to the reduction in the number of variables considered and the narrowing of evaluation criteria. The system cannot sustain complexity when time is limited. It reduces the dimensionality of the decision to a manageable subset. This simplification alters the decision output. The resulting choice is shaped not only by the available information, but by the constraints that determined which information could be processed.

Reduced evaluation increases the probability of misalignment. Misalignment occurs when the decision does not fully correspond to the system's constraints, exposures, or long-term trajectory. Under compressed time, the system lacks the capacity to fully test this alignment. It proceeds with partial validation. The likelihood that unexamined variables will influence the outcome increases. This is not a failure of logic. It is a consequence of insufficient evaluation relative to system complexity.

Financial pressure introduces a different form of constraint, centered on liquidity. Liquidity represents the system's ability to absorb variation over time. When liquidity is low, the system has limited capacity to sustain operations without immediate inflows. This condition reduces the range of feasible decisions. Options that require delay, buffering, or staged execution become less accessible. The system must operate within a narrower set of alternatives that can be executed with available resources.

Low liquidity reduces optionality by eliminating pathways that depend on time. Decisions that might otherwise be evaluated over extended intervals must be resolved quickly because the system cannot maintain its position without immediate action. This compression of options is not a function of preference. It is a structural limitation imposed by the system's inability to sustain delay. The decision space contracts to those options that can be executed within the remaining liquidity window.

As liquidity declines, decisions become increasingly reactive. Reactivity refers to the system's orientation toward immediate stabilization rather than directional alignment. When buffer capacity is low, the system prioritizes actions that address current deficits or exposures. It cannot allocate resources toward options that would improve long-term positioning if those options require short-term tolerance. The system's response becomes anchored to present constraints rather than future trajectory.

Financial pressure narrows the feasible decision space in a way that is both quantitative and qualitative. Quantitatively, fewer options remain available. Qualitatively, the nature of the remaining options shifts. They are more likely to involve trade-offs that preserve immediate function at the expense of future flexibility. This transformation of the decision space alters the type of decisions the system can produce. It is not selecting from the same set of alternatives under different conditions. It is selecting from a reduced and structurally altered set.

Liquidity determines tolerance for delay and evaluation. When liquidity is sufficient, the system can extend decision windows, gather additional information, and stage execution. When liquidity is constrained, these capabilities are removed. The system must act within shorter intervals and with less information. The absence of liquidity therefore translates directly into increased pressure on decision-making. It compresses both time and information simultaneously.

Under constrained liquidity, decisions are often made under unfavorable conditions. Unfavorable conditions refer to environments where the system lacks the capacity to absorb error or delay. The system may be required to commit to actions before full evaluation is possible, or to accept options that are suboptimal relative to those that would be available under less constrained conditions. This does not reflect a change in decision intent. It reflects a change in the environment that limits what can be achieved through decision-making.

Emotional compression emerges as an internal response to these external pressures. It is not separate from the system's structure. It is a reflection of how the system processes constraint when time, liquidity, and exposure converge. Emotional compression reduces the effective cognitive bandwidth available for decision-making. Bandwidth refers to the system's capacity to process information, maintain multiple variables in consideration, and sustain evaluation over time.

When pressure increases, cognitive bandwidth is reduced. The system reallocates resources toward managing immediate demands, leaving fewer resources available for extended evaluation. This reduction is structural. It follows from the interaction between external constraint and internal capacity. The system cannot maintain the same level of analytical depth under high pressure as it can under stable conditions. The decision process is therefore altered not only by external limits, but by the system's internal response to those limits.

Emotional states influence decision pacing and evaluation depth. Under compression, pacing accelerates. Decisions are made more quickly because the system cannot sustain prolonged evaluation. At the same time, depth decreases because fewer variables can be processed within the available bandwidth. This combination leads to a narrowing of focus. The system concentrates on a limited set of factors, often those most immediately relevant to the pressure being experienced.

Emotional compression is not an anomaly. It is a structural response to constraint. When the system is subjected to overlapping pressures, its internal processing adjusts accordingly. This adjustment is consistent across instances of high pressure. It reflects the system's adaptation to operating under reduced capacity. Treating this response as an irregularity obscures its role as a predictable component of decision behavior under constraint.

Emotional load interacts with time and financial pressure. When time is compressed and liquidity is low, the system experiences multiple constraints simultaneously. These constraints reinforce each other. Reduced time increases urgency, which heightens internal compression. Low liquidity increases exposure, which further narrows decision options and increases pressure. The interaction of these factors produces a compounded effect, where both external and internal conditions limit evaluation.

Compression reduces the consistency of decision processes. Consistency refers to the system's ability to apply the same structural approach across different decision instances. Under stable conditions, the process can maintain coherence. Under pressure, variations in available time, capacity, and exposure lead to variations in how decisions are made. The system adapts to each instance of constraint, resulting in less uniform application of its decision structure.

Urgency and importance represent two distinct dimensions of decision-making. Urgency is defined by time sensitivity. It reflects how quickly a decision must be made to avoid immediate consequences. Importance is defined by structural impact. It reflects how significantly a decision affects the system's long-term trajectory and stability. These dimensions do not necessarily align. A decision can be urgent without being structurally significant, and significant without being immediately urgent.

Pressure causes urgency to override importance. When time is compressed and exposure is elevated, the system prioritizes decisions that must be resolved quickly. This prioritization is not based on the long-term impact of the decision, but on the immediacy of its consequences. As a result, decisions that are structurally significant but not immediately time-sensitive may be deferred. The system allocates its limited capacity to resolving urgent issues, even if they do not materially alter the system's trajectory.

This reallocation leads to misprioritization. Attention is directed toward decisions that are visible through their immediacy, rather than those that shape the system's structural position. Over time, this pattern can alter the trajectory. Decisions that would maintain alignment with system constraints may be consistently deferred, while decisions that address immediate pressures are repeatedly prioritized. The cumulative effect is a shift in direction that is not immediately apparent through individual decision outcomes.

Urgent decisions are not inherently more significant. Their urgency arises from time constraint, not from structural impact. When the system treats urgency as a proxy for importance, it misinterprets the nature of the decision. This misinterpretation is reinforced under pressure because the system lacks the capacity to fully evaluate structural significance. It relies on immediacy as a guide, which simplifies prioritization but distorts alignment.

Importance is often deferred under high-pressure conditions because it does not demand immediate resolution. Decisions that shape long-term structure may not present immediate consequences if left unaddressed. In a compressed environment, these decisions are postponed in favor of those that require immediate action. This deferral is not a deliberate neglect. It is a consequence of limited capacity and competing demands.

Misprioritization alters trajectory over time. Each instance of deferring structurally significant decisions contributes to a gradual shift in the system's position. The system may maintain short-term functionality by addressing urgent issues, but its alignment with long-term stability can deteriorate. This deterioration is not visible through isolated decisions. It emerges through the accumulation of prioritization patterns shaped by pressure.

Time pressure, financial pressure, and emotional compression operate as interconnected constraints that reshape the decision environment. Each form of pressure reduces the system's ability to conduct comprehensive evaluation. Time pressure limits duration, financial pressure limits optionality, and emotional compression limits processing capacity. Together, they create a condition in which decisions are made with reduced information, shortened evaluation windows, and constrained alternatives.

As these constraints tighten, evaluation quality declines across all dimensions. Evaluation quality refers to the system's ability to assess alignment between decisions and its structural conditions. Under pressure, this assessment is incomplete. The system cannot fully account for all variables, cannot explore all alternatives, and cannot sustain the analysis required to ensure alignment. The resulting decisions are therefore more likely to diverge from the system's optimal trajectory.

Error rate increases as a function of this compression. Error is not defined as an unfavorable outcome. It is defined as misalignment between the decision and the system's structure, including its constraints, capacities, and exposures. Under pressure, the probability of such misalignment increases because the system lacks the conditions necessary to fully validate its decisions. This increase is not random. It follows directly from the reduction in evaluation quality.

Because pressure is a recurring condition within financial systems, the increase in error is not isolated to singular events. Decisions are repeatedly made under compressed conditions. Each instance carries a higher probability of misalignment. Over time, these misalignments accumulate. The system's trajectory is shaped by a sequence of decisions produced under pressure, each contributing to directional drift.

This accumulation introduces instability. The system does not fail because of a single error, but because repeated pressure-induced misalignments reposition it relative to its structural thresholds. As the system moves closer to these thresholds, its tolerance for further error decreases. Subsequent decisions, made under continued pressure, have a greater impact on stability. The interaction between pressure and trajectory creates a feedback loop, where increased pressure leads to increased error, which in turn increases exposure to further pressure.

The Decision Pressure Mechanism describes this process. Pressure compresses the conditions under which decisions are made. This compression reduces evaluation quality, increases the probability of misalignment, and alters prioritization. These effects are structural. They arise from the interaction between constraint and system capacity. As decisions are made under these conditions, their cumulative impact determines whether the system maintains stability or moves toward instability.

The Information Gap Mechanism

Information is often treated as a prerequisite for decision-making, with the implicit assumption that sufficient inputs can be assembled before action is taken. Within a financial system, this assumption does not hold. Information is not fully available at the moment it is required, nor does it arrive in a complete and synchronized form. Decisions are made within conditions where inputs are missing, delayed, or only partially observable. This condition is not an occasional disruption. It is the baseline environment in which decisions operate.

Missing information refers to inputs that are not available at the time a decision must be made. These inputs may exist in the system or in the external environment, but they are not accessible within the decision window. The absence may be due to inherent uncertainty, lack of visibility, or the inability to measure certain variables in real time. Regardless of the cause, the result is the same: the decision must proceed without incorporating these inputs. The evaluation state is therefore incomplete from the outset.

Delayed information introduces a different form of incompleteness. In this case, inputs do exist and are eventually observable, but they arrive after the decision point has passed. The system does not have access to these inputs during evaluation, but they become visible in subsequent periods. This creates a temporal gap between decision and information.

The decision is made under one set of observable conditions, while the full informational context becomes apparent only later.

Both missing and delayed information create incomplete evaluation states. The system does not have a fully resolved view of the variables influencing the decision. It operates within a partial representation of reality, where certain factors are unknown and others are only partially understood. This incompleteness is not corrected before the decision is executed. The system cannot pause indefinitely to wait for information that may not arrive within the required timeframe. The decision must proceed despite these gaps.

The timing of information directly affects decision quality. When relevant inputs are missing, the system cannot incorporate them into its evaluation, increasing the likelihood that the decision will not fully align with the system's structure or exposure conditions. When information is delayed, the system may later observe outcomes that appear inconsistent with the initial evaluation. This inconsistency is not necessarily due to flawed reasoning. It reflects the fact that the decision was made without access to information that only became available afterward.

Delayed information also alters interpretation after the fact. Once additional inputs become visible, the system can reconstruct the decision context with greater completeness. This reconstruction creates the appearance that the decision could have been made differently if the information had been available earlier. However, this interpretation is retrospective. At the moment of decision, the system operated within a different informational boundary. The gap between these two states—decision-time information and post-decision information—creates a divergence between how decisions are experienced and how they are later evaluated.

Within incomplete information environments, distinguishing between signal and noise becomes structurally complex. Signal refers to information that materially affects the decision's alignment with system conditions. It is information that changes the evaluation of alternatives in a meaningful way. Noise refers to inputs that do not materially alter the decision, either because they are irrelevant or because their impact is negligible relative to other variables. In an ideal environment, signal can be isolated and noise can be filtered. Under incomplete conditions, this separation is unstable.

The difficulty arises because the system does not have full visibility into which inputs are relevant. When information is incomplete, the system cannot definitively classify inputs as signal or noise. Variables that appear significant may later prove to be inconsequential, while variables that appear minor may later have substantial impact. The absence of complete information prevents accurate classification at the time of decision.

Noise can therefore appear as signal under uncertainty. Inputs that are available may be given disproportionate weight simply because they are visible, not because they are structurally important. The system may rely on these inputs to construct its evaluation, even if they do not materially influence the outcome. This reliance is not a deliberate misinterpretation. It is a consequence of operating within a limited information set where available inputs are used as proxies for a more complete understanding.

Excess information does not resolve this condition. Increasing the volume of inputs does not guarantee that signal can be identified more effectively. When the system is constrained by time and capacity, additional information can increase complexity without improving clarity. The system must still filter inputs within its available bandwidth. Under pressure, this filtering process is itself constrained. The system cannot fully evaluate the relevance of each input, leading to a mixture of signal and noise within the decision process.

Filtering is therefore structurally limited. The system's ability to distinguish relevant from irrelevant information is bounded by its capacity to process inputs and the time available for evaluation. When these constraints are tight, filtering becomes less precise. The system may include noise in its evaluation or exclude relevant signals. This imprecision is not an anomaly. It is a direct consequence of operating under incomplete information and constrained capacity.

Within this environment, false certainty can emerge. False certainty refers to the perception that the decision context is sufficiently understood when, in fact, it is not. The system constructs a coherent interpretation of the available information and treats it as a complete representation of the environment. This perception does not require full information. It can arise from partial inputs that appear internally consistent.

Incomplete inputs can still produce confident conclusions. The system integrates the information it has into a structured interpretation, filling gaps implicitly through assumptions or inferred relationships. These inferences may not be explicitly recognized as such. They become embedded within the evaluation as if they were grounded in observable data. The resulting decision appears to be based on a complete understanding, even though key variables remain unobserved.

Systems may interpret partial information as complete because the evaluation process requires a resolved state. A decision cannot be executed in a state of indefinite ambiguity. The system must arrive at a conclusion, even if the underlying information is incomplete. This necessity leads to the closure of the evaluation process before full informational resolution is achieved. The system behaves as if the available information is sufficient, because it must act within the constraints of time and capacity.

False certainty reduces awareness of exposure. When the system perceives its understanding as complete, it does not account for the potential impact of unknown variables. Exposure refers to the system's sensitivity to outcomes that are influenced by factors not fully incorporated into the decision. If these factors are not recognized as missing, their potential impact is not considered. The system's assessment of risk is therefore understated relative to the actual conditions.

Confidence is not a proxy for completeness. A decision can be made with high confidence based on a coherent but incomplete interpretation of available information. This confidence reflects the internal consistency of the evaluation, not the completeness of the inputs. The system's perception of certainty is therefore decoupled from the actual informational state. High confidence does not indicate that all relevant variables have been accounted for. It indicates that the system has resolved its evaluation within the constraints it faces.

Overconfidence arises when there is a misalignment between perceived and actual information completeness. The system believes it has sufficient information to make an informed decision, while in reality, significant gaps remain. This misalignment is not necessarily the result of deliberate overestimation. It emerges from the structure of the decision environment. When information is limited, the system relies more heavily on internal assumptions to fill gaps. These assumptions are integrated into the evaluation without always being recognized as provisional.

Limited information increases reliance on internal models. The system uses prior knowledge, inferred relationships, and simplified representations to compensate for missing inputs. These models provide a framework for interpreting available information and projecting outcomes. However, they are constructed under the same constraints that limit information. They may not fully capture the complexity of the environment. The system's dependence on these models increases as information becomes more incomplete.

As the system fills gaps implicitly, the distinction between observed and assumed information becomes less clear. Assumptions are treated as part of the informational base, even though they are not directly supported by observable inputs. This integration creates a perception of completeness that does not correspond to the actual informational state. The system's confidence in its evaluation increases, not because information has improved, but because the gaps have been internally resolved.

Overconfidence is therefore a structural outcome of operating under incomplete information. It does not require a change in behavior or disposition. It emerges from the necessity of making decisions within constrained informational environments. The system must act, and in doing so, it constructs a sense of certainty sufficient to support that action. This certainty is not externally validated. It is internally generated within the bounds of the available information.

Uncertainty does not reduce the occurrence of decision-making. The system cannot defer decisions until uncertainty is eliminated. Instead, uncertainty shifts how decisions are performed. The evaluation process incorporates assumptions more heavily, relies on partial inputs, and operates within a narrower informational frame. The presence of uncertainty changes the structure of decision-making without reducing its frequency.

Missing information, difficulty in distinguishing signal from noise, and the emergence of false certainty combine to create a condition of structural ambiguity. Ambiguity refers to the absence of full informational resolution. The system does not operate with precise, fully defined states. It operates within ranges of possible conditions, where the exact configuration of variables is not fully known.

Structural ambiguity is persistent. It is not resolved through additional effort alone, because the limitations are embedded in the timing, availability, and processing of information. The system must function within this ambiguity. Decisions are made based on ranges, probabilities, and partial representations, rather than on complete and certain inputs. The evaluation process produces conclusions that are sufficient for action, but not fully resolved in an absolute sense.

Within this condition, decisions do not correspond to exact points in a fully known system. They correspond to positions within a range of possible states. The system selects a direction based on its interpretation of this range, not on a definitive understanding of all variables. The resulting trajectory reflects this ambiguity. It incorporates the effects of decisions made under incomplete information, each contributing to the system's evolution.

Ambiguity cannot be eliminated as a prerequisite for decision-making. The system does not have the capacity to wait for full informational resolution, nor is such resolution consistently attainable. Instead, the system operates continuously within ambiguous conditions. The structure of decision-making must therefore accommodate this reality. Decisions are not made after uncertainty is removed. They are made within it.

This condition affects downstream decision consistency and stability. When each decision is made within a different configuration of missing, delayed, and distorted information, the consistency of the decision process is challenged. The system may apply similar structural rules, but the inputs vary in completeness and clarity. This variation introduces dispersion in decision outputs, even when the underlying process remains constant.

Over time, the accumulation of decisions made under structural ambiguity shapes the system's trajectory. Each decision reflects an interpretation of incomplete information. As these interpretations compound, the system moves through states that may not have been fully anticipated at any single decision point. Stability is therefore not determined by the elimination of ambiguity, but by how the system navigates within it.

The Inevitable Error Mechanism

Error is often interpreted as a deviation from correct decision-making, implying that it arises when the system fails to operate as intended. Within a financial system, this interpretation is incomplete. Error is not solely the result of flawed reasoning or improper execution. It is an inherent output of a system operating under constraint, pressure, and incomplete information. Decisions are made within environments that do not allow full alignment between evaluation and reality. The resulting misalignment is not exceptional. It is structural.

Error can be defined as the difference between the system's interpretation of conditions at the time of decision and the actual configuration of those conditions as they unfold. This difference arises because the system does not have complete access to all relevant variables, cannot fully model their interactions, and must act within limited time. Even when the decision process is internally consistent and structurally sound, the alignment between decision and outcome is not guaranteed. The system operates on representations of reality, not on reality in its entirety.

This establishes the presence of a baseline error rate. A baseline error rate represents the level of misalignment that persists even when the system is functioning as designed. It is not the result of malfunction. It is the result of operating conditions that prevent perfect correspondence between decision inputs and system outcomes. Constraints limit evaluation, pressure compresses decision windows, and information gaps restrict visibility. These conditions ensure that some degree of error is always present.

No decision system operates at zero error. The concept of a fully aligned decision—one that perfectly anticipates all variables and outcomes—is not achievable within real-world conditions. Even in stable environments, where variability is reduced and constraints are less severe, the system still lacks complete information and unlimited capacity. Decisions made under these conditions may appear accurate, but they still contain elements of approximation. The absence of visible error does not indicate its absence in structure. It indicates that the system has not encountered conditions that expose it.

Constraints, pressure, and information gaps interact to produce persistent error. Constraints limit what can be evaluated, pressure reduces the time available for evaluation, and information gaps prevent full visibility into relevant variables. These factors do not occur independently. They overlap and reinforce each other, creating an environment in which decisions are necessarily made with incomplete alignment. The resulting error is not incidental. It is embedded in the process through which decisions are generated.

Error frequency is therefore structural. It does not depend on isolated events or individual decision instances. It is a characteristic of the system's operating conditions. Each decision carries a probability of misalignment that is determined by the constraints present at the time of evaluation. As these conditions persist, the occurrence of error becomes continuous rather than occasional. The system produces a stream of decisions, each containing some degree of approximation relative to actual conditions.

Randomness further complicates the relationship between decisions and outcomes. Randomness refers to variation in outcomes that cannot be fully attributed to the structure of the decision process. It arises from external factors, interactions between variables, and fluctuations that are not predictable at the time of decision. Even when the decision process is consistent, randomness can produce different results across similar instances.

Outcomes can diverge from expectations because the system operates within an environment that is not fully deterministic. External conditions change, interactions between variables evolve, and events occur that are not captured within the decision model. These factors introduce variability that is independent of the decision structure. As a result, the same decision, applied under similar conditions, can lead to different outcomes.

Identical decisions do not guarantee identical results. The system may apply the same process, evaluate the same inputs, and select the same option, yet the outcome may differ due to variations in external conditions. This divergence is not evidence of inconsistency within the decision process. It is evidence of variability within the environment. The system interacts with factors that are not fully controlled or predictable, and these interactions influence the result.

Outcome variability does not imply process instability. A stable decision process can produce a range of outcomes due to randomness. Conversely, an unstable process can occasionally produce favorable outcomes if external conditions align. The relationship between process and outcome is therefore probabilistic rather than deterministic. Evaluating the process based solely on outcomes can obscure its structural properties, as variability may mask underlying consistency or inconsistency.

Randomness obscures the evaluation of decision quality. When outcomes vary independently of the decision structure, it becomes difficult to attribute results to the process itself. Favorable outcomes may be interpreted as evidence of high-quality decisions, even if they occurred under favorable external conditions. Unfavorable outcomes may be interpreted as evidence of poor decisions, even if they resulted from adverse variability. The presence of randomness introduces ambiguity into the assessment of whether decisions are aligned with system conditions.

Forecasting introduces another source of error. Forecasting is the process of projecting future conditions based on current information and assumed relationships between variables. It is necessary because decisions often involve future consequences. The system must estimate how conditions will evolve in order to select a direction. However, forecasting operates under the same constraints that affect all decision-making: incomplete information, limited capacity, and environmental variability.

Forecasts are constructed within uncertainty. The system does not have full visibility into future states, nor can it predict all interactions between variables. It must rely on models that simplify the environment, using available data to infer likely outcomes. These models are approximations. They cannot fully capture the complexity of the system or the range of possible future conditions. As a result, forecasts inherently contain error.

Projections cannot fully represent system complexity because the number of interacting variables exceeds the system's capacity to model them. Even when significant effort is applied to forecasting, the resulting projections remain simplified representations of a more complex reality. Certain variables are included, others are excluded, and interactions are often linearized or approximated. These simplifications are necessary for the model to be usable, but they introduce divergence between the forecast and actual outcomes.

Forecasting error is therefore unavoidable. It does not arise solely from incorrect assumptions or insufficient effort. It arises from the structural limitation that future conditions cannot be fully known or modeled. The system must make decisions based on these imperfect projections, accepting that the actual outcome will differ to some degree from the forecast. This difference contributes to the baseline error rate inherent in the system.

Forward-looking decisions are inherently approximate. They rely on projections that are subject to uncertainty and variability. The system does not have access to future states at the time of decision. It constructs an expected trajectory based on available information, but this trajectory is not exact. The decision aligns with the forecasted state, not with the actual state that will unfold. The divergence between these two states is a source of error that cannot be eliminated.

Baseline error, randomness, and imperfect forecasting operate together to ensure that error is a persistent feature of decision systems. Each component contributes to misalignment between decision and outcome. Baseline error arises from constraints and incomplete information, randomness introduces variability independent of the decision process, and forecasting error reflects the inability to fully predict future conditions. These factors are not independent. They interact to shape the system's behavior.

Because these sources of error are structural, they cannot be removed through increased effort or refinement of individual decisions. Improving evaluation within the constraints of the system does not eliminate the constraints themselves. Additional analysis does not remove uncertainty, nor does it eliminate variability in outcomes. The system can adjust how it processes information, but it cannot operate outside the conditions that produce error.

The implication is that systems must be structured to absorb error. Absorption refers to the system's ability to continue functioning despite misalignment between decisions and outcomes. It does not require that error be eliminated. It requires that the system can tolerate the presence of error without transitioning into instability. This tolerance is determined by the system's configuration, including its capacity, exposure levels, and proximity to structural thresholds.

Absorption operates through the system's ability to accommodate deviations without cascading failure. When a decision produces an outcome that differs from expectation, the system must be able to adjust without exceeding its constraints. This adjustment may involve reallocating resources, absorbing losses, or modifying subsequent decisions. The system's structure determines whether these adjustments are possible within its tolerance range.

Stability therefore depends on error tolerance, not on error avoidance. A system that requires perfect alignment between decisions and outcomes is inherently fragile, because such alignment cannot be consistently achieved. A system that can absorb a range of misalignments can maintain stability even when individual decisions produce imperfect results. The focus shifts from eliminating error to managing its impact within the system.

As decisions are made over time, the accumulation of error becomes a critical factor in system behavior. Each instance of misalignment contributes to the system's trajectory, altering its position relative to constraints and thresholds. The system does not experience error as isolated events. It experiences the cumulative effect of repeated approximations. The ability to absorb individual errors does not guarantee the ability to absorb their accumulation.

The interaction between error and system trajectory introduces a dynamic element to stability. As the system moves through different states, its tolerance for additional error may change. A system with sufficient capacity and low exposure may absorb repeated errors without approaching instability. A system operating near its limits may have little tolerance for further misalignment. In such conditions, even small errors can have amplified effects.

The Inevitable Error Mechanism defines this structural reality. Error is not an anomaly to be eliminated, but a constant output of decision systems operating under real-world conditions. It arises from the interaction of constraints, variability, and incomplete information. Its presence is continuous, its frequency is structural, and its impact depends on the system's ability to absorb it. Understanding this mechanism reframes the role of decisions within the system. Decisions do not produce perfect alignment. They produce approximations that interact with a variable environment. Stability emerges not from the absence of error, but from the system's capacity to remain intact as error accumulates over time.

The Reversibility Mechanism

Decisions differ not only in their immediate effects but in how those effects can be altered once they have been applied to the system. This distinction is not defined by the visible scale of the decision or by how it is perceived at the moment it is made. It is defined by reversibility. A reversible decision is one whose effects can be undone or materially altered with limited cost, allowing the system to return to a prior or alternative state without significant structural disruption. An irreversible decision is one whose effects cannot be undone without incurring substantial loss, or cannot be undone at all, embedding its consequences into the system's configuration.

Reversibility determines structural impact because it defines whether the system retains the ability to adjust its trajectory after a decision has been executed. When a decision is reversible, the system is not permanently committed to the direction it introduces. If the outcome diverges from expectation, the system can modify or reverse the decision, restoring alignment or shifting to a different path. The presence of this corrective capacity reduces the long-term influence of any single decision, even if its short-term effects are pronounced.

Irreversible decisions operate differently. Once executed, their effects become embedded within the system's structure. The system cannot return to its prior state without absorbing significant cost, or it may be unable to return at all. This embedding alters the system's configuration in a lasting way, changing its available paths and future conditions. The impact of such decisions is not limited to their immediate outcome. It extends across all subsequent states, as the system continues to operate within the constraints introduced by the decision.

The distinction between reversible and irreversible decisions is not determined by perceived importance. A decision that appears minor may be irreversible if it alters the system in a way that cannot be undone. A decision that appears significant may be reversible if the system retains the capacity to adjust or reverse it without substantial consequence. Structural impact is therefore determined by the ability to reverse, not by subjective evaluation of scale or consequence at the moment of decision.

Reversible decisions allow correction after error. When misalignment occurs, the system can adjust its position, reducing the accumulation of error over time. This capacity does not eliminate error, but it limits its persistence. The system can incorporate feedback from outcomes and modify its trajectory accordingly. The presence of reversibility creates a dynamic in which decisions can be iterated upon, refined, or replaced as conditions evolve.

Irreversible decisions do not provide this flexibility. Once misalignment is introduced, it cannot be removed through reversal. The system must operate within the new configuration, carrying the effects of the decision forward. Any adjustment must occur within the constraints imposed by the irreversible change. This increases the structural weight of the decision, as its consequences extend beyond the initial moment and influence all subsequent states.

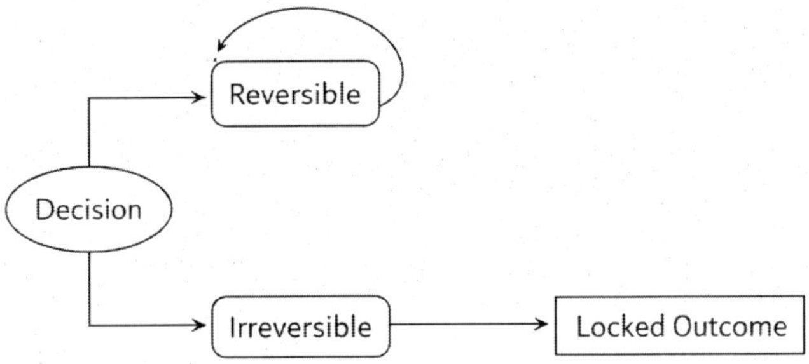

[Figure 1: Reversible vs Irreversible Decision Tree]

The structural difference between reversible and irreversible decisions becomes visible when the system's trajectory is represented as a branching process. Reversible decisions create branches that include loops, allowing the system to return to prior nodes or shift between adjacent paths. Irreversible decisions create branches that terminate in endpoints from which return is not possible. The system moves forward from these endpoints along constrained paths, with no direct mechanism for reversal.

Optionality is the system's ability to maintain multiple possible future paths. It represents the range of trajectories that remain accessible given the system's current configuration. Optionality is not static. It is shaped by decisions, particularly by their degree of reversibility. When optionality is high, the system retains flexibility. It can adjust direction in response to new information, changing conditions, or observed misalignment. When optionality is low, the system is confined to a narrower set of paths, limiting its ability to adapt.

Reversible decisions preserve optionality because they do not eliminate future paths. Even after a decision is executed, the system retains the ability to move to alternative states. The presence of reversibility ensures that the system is not fully committed to a single trajectory. It can explore different directions, evaluate outcomes, and adjust without permanently constraining its future. This preservation of optionality functions as a structural buffer against uncertainty, allowing the system to respond to variability without being locked into a single course.

Irreversible decisions collapse optionality. By embedding a particular configuration into the system, they remove alternative paths that would have been available prior to the decision. The system's future becomes constrained by the new structure. Options that depended on the previous state are no longer accessible, and new options may be limited by the constraints introduced. The reduction in optionality is not always immediately visible. It becomes apparent as the system attempts to respond to changing conditions and finds that certain paths are no longer available.

Optionality functions as a buffer because it allows the system to absorb error and variability without being forced into unfavorable states. When multiple paths remain open, the system can adjust its trajectory in response to new information. If one path proves misaligned, another can be pursued. This flexibility reduces the impact of individual errors and allows the system to maintain stability across a range of conditions.

The loss of optionality increases exposure to error. When the system is confined to a limited set of paths, any misalignment within those paths has a greater impact. The system cannot easily adjust or redirect its trajectory. It must operate within the constraints of its reduced option set. This increases the sensitivity of outcomes to error, as there are fewer mechanisms available to correct or mitigate its effects.

Path dependency emerges from the accumulation of decisions, particularly those that are irreversible. Path dependency refers to the condition in which the system's current state and future possibilities are determined by the sequence of decisions that preceded it. The system does not operate in an abstract space of possibilities. It operates within a trajectory shaped by its history. Each decision modifies this trajectory, and irreversible decisions have a disproportionate influence on how tightly the system is bound to its past.

Irreversible decisions lock the system into specific trajectories by embedding constraints that cannot be removed. Once such a decision is made, the system's future states are conditioned on that change. The range of feasible decisions that follow is altered. Some options are eliminated, while others become more or less accessible depending on the new configuration. The system's path is therefore not only influenced by the decision, but constrained by it.

Future decisions are made within the context created by prior irreversible choices. The system cannot evaluate options independently of its current state, and that state reflects the accumulation of past decisions. When irreversible decisions dominate the sequence, the system becomes increasingly constrained. Each new decision must operate within a narrower set of possibilities, shaped by the constraints that have already been embedded.

Reversibility affects how tightly the system is bound to its past. When decisions are predominantly reversible, the system retains the ability to adjust its trajectory and reduce the influence of prior states. Path dependency is present, but it is less rigid. The system can modify its position, reintroduce optionality, and alter its direction. When decisions are predominantly irreversible, path dependency becomes more rigid. The system is increasingly constrained by its history, and its ability to deviate from established trajectories is reduced.

Path dependency accumulates through irreversible actions. Each irreversible decision adds a layer of constraint, narrowing the system's future paths. The accumulation is not linear. As constraints build, their interaction can produce nonlinear effects, where the system's flexibility is reduced more rapidly than the number of irreversible decisions might suggest. The system may reach a point where its trajectory is highly constrained, and its ability to adapt to new conditions is limited.

Reversibility, optionality, and path dependency are interconnected components of the system's structure. Reversibility preserves optionality, allowing the system to maintain flexibility. Irreversibility reduces optionality, increasing path dependency. As path dependency increases, the system becomes more sensitive to its past decisions and less able to adjust its trajectory. These dynamics determine how decisions influence long-term stability.

Irreversible decisions carry disproportionate structural weight because they permanently alter the system's configuration and eliminate future paths. Their impact is not confined to the moment of execution. It extends across all subsequent states, shaping the system's evolution over time. The system's exposure increases when reversibility is reduced, as it becomes more dependent on the accuracy of decisions that cannot be corrected.

Irreversible exposure can be defined as the portion of the system's trajectory that is determined by decisions that cannot be undone. This exposure represents a form of structural commitment. The system is bound to the consequences of these decisions, regardless of how conditions change. As irreversible exposure increases, the system's tolerance for error decreases. The inability to reverse decisions means that misalignment persists and accumulates.

System stability depends on how irreversible decisions accumulate over time. A system that accumulates irreversible exposure rapidly may become constrained and fragile, as its ability to adjust is reduced. A system that maintains a balance between reversible and irreversible decisions retains greater flexibility, allowing it to respond to variability and correct misalignment. The structure of decision reversibility therefore plays a central role in determining how the system evolves.

As decisions continue to shape the system, the management of their structural impact becomes critical. The distinction between reversible and irreversible decisions defines how the system can respond to error, preserve optionality, and manage path dependency. The accumulation of irreversible exposure introduces constraints that influence all future decisions, altering the system's trajectory in ways that cannot be undone.

Understanding the Reversibility Mechanism reframes how decisions are evaluated within a financial system. The focus shifts from the immediate outcome of a decision to its structural effect on the system's ability to adjust. Decisions are not equivalent in their long-term influence. Those that can be reversed allow the system to remain flexible and adaptive. Those that cannot be reversed embed their consequences, shaping the system's path in a lasting way.

As the system continues to operate, the interaction between reversibility and trajectory determines how it responds to uncertainty, variability, and error. Decisions that preserve optionality allow for adjustment and correction, while decisions that eliminate optionality increase exposure and constrain future states. The balance between these forces defines the system's capacity to maintain stability over time.

The Downside Sensitivity Mechanism

Decisions are often evaluated through the lens of likelihood, where the primary question is how probable a given outcome is. This framing places emphasis on frequency—how often a particular result is expected to occur within a defined set of conditions. Likelihood, in this sense, becomes the dominant measure of evaluation. However, within a financial system, likelihood alone does not determine the structural impact of a decision. The system is not shaped by how often outcomes occur, but by how much those outcomes alter its configuration when they do occur.

Magnitude defines this structural impact. Magnitude refers to the scale of change introduced into the system when an outcome materializes. It measures how far the system is displaced from its prior state, how much capacity is consumed or lost, and how the system's trajectory is altered. While likelihood describes frequency, magnitude describes consequence. These two dimensions operate independently. An outcome can be highly likely with minimal impact, or highly unlikely with substantial impact. The system's behavior is determined by the interaction between these dimensions, but not symmetrically.

Evaluation that prioritizes likelihood alone assumes that frequent outcomes dominate system behavior. This assumption holds only when magnitude is relatively uniform across outcomes. In most financial systems, magnitude is not uniform. Certain outcomes carry disproportionately large effects relative to their probability. These outcomes may occur infrequently, but when they do, they alter the system in ways that cannot be offset by the accumulation of smaller, more frequent results.

Low-probability, high-impact events dominate system outcomes because their magnitude exceeds the system's capacity to absorb them without structural change. When such an event occurs, it can reduce liquidity, increase rigidity, or shift exposure in a way that redefines the system's operating range. The system does not average this impact across time. It incorporates it immediately into its structure. The effect persists, influencing all subsequent decisions and outcomes.

Likelihood without magnitude is therefore an incomplete evaluation. A decision that appears favorable based on high-probability, low-impact outcomes may still introduce exposure to low-probability, high-impact loss. The system's sensitivity to this exposure is not captured by likelihood alone. It is determined by the potential displacement introduced by the outcome if it occurs. This displacement defines the system's vulnerability.

Asymmetry arises when gains and losses of similar magnitude do not produce equivalent structural effects. In a symmetric system, a gain of a given size would offset a loss of the same size, restoring the system to its prior state. Financial systems do not operate symmetrically. Losses and gains interact differently with the system's structure. A loss reduces capacity, alters exposure, and may introduce constraints that did not previously exist. A gain increases capacity, but does not necessarily remove constraints that have already been embedded.

Loss asymmetry means that negative outcomes have a greater structural effect than positive outcomes of equivalent size. When a loss occurs, it may reduce the system's ability to sustain future variability. It can compress liquidity, increase obligation density relative to capacity, and move the system closer to structural thresholds. These changes alter the system's configuration in a way that cannot be fully reversed by a subsequent gain of the same magnitude.

Recovery from loss requires a greater relative gain because the system operates on a reduced base after the loss occurs. If a system loses a portion of its capacity, the remaining capacity must generate a proportionally larger gain to restore the original level. This relationship creates a nonlinear dynamic, where losses compound more aggressively than gains. The system's trajectory is therefore more sensitive to negative deviations than to positive ones.

Negative outcomes compound differently because they interact with constraints. A loss may increase the system's rigidity, reduce its flexibility, and limit its ability to respond to future changes. These effects accumulate, creating a condition where subsequent losses have amplified impact. Gains, while beneficial, do not necessarily reverse these accumulated constraints. They may improve the system's position, but the structural changes introduced by prior losses may persist.

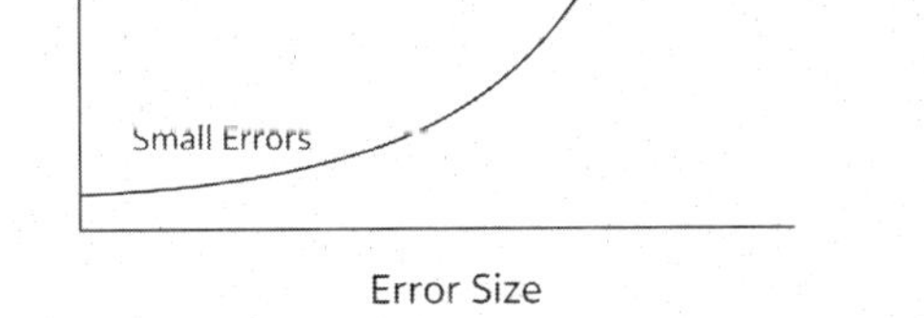

[Figure 2: Downside Impact Curve]

This asymmetry can be represented as a curve where negative deviations produce larger structural displacement than equivalent positive deviations. The system's response to loss is steeper and more pronounced, reflecting its sensitivity to downside events. Positive deviations produce improvement, but their effect is more gradual and does not fully counterbalance the displacement caused by losses. The curve illustrates that the system's behavior is not linear with respect to gains and losses.

Systems are therefore more sensitive to losses than to gains. This sensitivity is not a function of preference or perception. It is a structural characteristic arising from how losses interact with capacity, exposure, and constraints. The system's stability depends on its ability to withstand negative deviations without crossing thresholds that alter its operating conditions. Gains contribute to stability, but they do not carry the same capacity to destabilize as losses do.

Fragility emerges from this sensitivity. Fragility can be defined as the degree to which a system is affected by downside events. A fragile system is one in which relatively small negative deviations can produce significant structural change. This condition is determined by the system's exposure to loss and its capacity to absorb it. When exposure is high relative to capacity, the system becomes more sensitive to negative outcomes.

Systems with high downside exposure are unstable because they operate close to their structural limits. In such systems, the margin between current conditions and failure thresholds is narrow. A large negative outcome, even if unlikely, can push the system beyond these thresholds. The system does not fail gradually. It transitions abruptly when the threshold is crossed. This transition is a function of exposure, not of frequency.

Fragility is revealed under stress rather than under normal conditions. In stable periods, the system may appear robust because negative outcomes do not occur, or their magnitude remains within the system's tolerance. This appearance is conditional. It reflects the absence of stress rather than the presence of resilience. When stress introduces larger or more frequent negative deviations, the system's sensitivity becomes visible. The underlying structure determines how it responds.

Exposure to large losses determines system resilience. A resilient system is one that can absorb significant negative deviations without undergoing structural failure. This absorption depends on the relationship between the magnitude of potential losses and the system's capacity. If the system's exposure includes outcomes that exceed its capacity to absorb them, resilience is reduced. The system becomes fragile, not because it is poorly designed in general, but because it is exposed to outcomes that it cannot withstand.

Fragility is structural, not situational. It does not arise solely from external conditions. It is embedded in the system's configuration, specifically in how exposure to downside events is distributed relative to capacity. External conditions may trigger the realization of negative outcomes, but the system's response is determined by its internal structure. Two systems exposed to the same external event may respond differently depending on their respective levels of fragility.

Magnitude, asymmetry, and fragility together define how downside events shape system behavior. Magnitude determines the scale of impact, asymmetry defines how that impact interacts with gains and losses, and fragility determines the system's sensitivity to that impact. These elements are interconnected. A system exposed to high-magnitude negative outcomes, combined with asymmetric loss dynamics and limited capacity, will exhibit high fragility.

Large downside events dominate long-term system behavior because they introduce structural changes that persist across time. Frequent small outcomes, even when positive, do not offset the impact of a single large negative event if that event alters the system's configuration. The system's trajectory is therefore influenced more by extreme deviations than by average conditions. Stability cannot be understood by examining typical outcomes alone. It must account for the potential impact of infrequent but significant losses.

Stability depends on limiting exposure to extreme loss because such losses have the capacity to move the system beyond its tolerance range. When this occurs, the system may experience a reduction in optionality, an increase in rigidity, or a shift in its operating constraints. These changes are not easily reversed. They redefine the system's future states and influence all subsequent decisions.

Downside sensitivity can be defined as the degree to which the system's trajectory is affected by negative outcomes. A system with high downside sensitivity will exhibit large changes in response to relatively small negative deviations. A system with lower sensitivity will absorb these deviations with less structural impact. This sensitivity is determined by the relationship between exposure and capacity, as well as by the asymmetry in how losses are processed.

Systems fail from large losses, not from small fluctuations. Small fluctuations may introduce variability, but they do not typically alter the system's structure if they remain within its tolerance range. Large losses, even if rare, have the capacity to breach this range. When they do, the system's behavior changes. It may enter a state where its prior configuration is no longer sustainable, leading to instability or failure.

The Downside Sensitivity Mechanism establishes that the structural importance of a decision is defined by its exposure to large negative outcomes. Decisions that introduce the possibility of significant loss carry greater weight than those associated with frequent but minor outcomes. This weight is not determined by how often the outcome occurs, but by how much it alters the system when it does.

As decisions accumulate, the system's exposure to downside events becomes a defining characteristic of its stability. Each decision contributes to the distribution of potential outcomes, shaping the range and magnitude of possible losses. The system's long-term behavior reflects this distribution. It is not the average outcome that determines stability, but the system's ability to withstand its worst outcomes.

Understanding this mechanism shifts the evaluation of decisions from frequency to consequence. It highlights that the system's trajectory is governed by its sensitivity to downside events, and that this sensitivity is embedded in its structure. The interaction between magnitude, asymmetry, and fragility defines how the system responds to negative deviations, and ultimately, whether it remains stable under stress.

The Decision Asymmetry Mechanism

A decision produces not a single outcome, but a distribution of possible outcomes. This distribution defines the decision's payoff structure. It includes the range of gains and losses that may occur, the frequency with which they occur, and the magnitude associated with each possibility. The system does not experience only the expected or average result of this distribution. It is exposed to the full range of outcomes, including those that occur infrequently but carry significant impact.

Within most financial systems, payoff structures are not evenly distributed. Gains and losses do not mirror each other in frequency or magnitude. A decision may produce a series of small positive outcomes under normal conditions, creating the appearance of stability or incremental progress. At the same time, it may contain the potential for a larger negative outcome that occurs less frequently but carries a disproportionate effect on the system. This uneven distribution defines asymmetry.

The presence of frequent small gains and rare large losses creates a structural imbalance. The system accumulates positive outcomes over time, but these gains do not offset the impact of a single large loss if that loss alters the system's configuration. The distribution is therefore skewed. The system's trajectory is not determined by the accumulation of gains alone, but by how those gains interact with the possibility of loss embedded within the same decision structure.

Payoff asymmetry determines structural risk because it defines how the system is exposed to extreme outcomes. A decision with symmetric outcomes—where gains and losses are similar in magnitude and frequency—affects the system in a predictable and balanced way. A decision with asymmetric outcomes introduces uneven exposure. The system may experience stability across many instances, but remains vulnerable to a single event that can offset accumulated gains and alter its trajectory.

Average outcomes obscure the shape of this distribution. When evaluation focuses on expected value or typical results, the influence of rare but significant outcomes is diluted. The system appears stable because the average outcome is positive or neutral. However, this average does not capture the structural impact of tail events. The distribution's shape—specifically the presence of large negative outcomes—determines how the system behaves over time.

Risk and reward are often framed as opposing forces that balance each other within a decision. Risk is typically associated with the possibility of loss, while reward is associated with the potential for gain. This framing assumes that these elements can be compared on a similar scale. Within asymmetric payoff structures, this assumption does not hold. Risk and reward are not equivalent because their structural effects differ.

Risk can be defined in terms of downside magnitude, representing the scale of loss that may occur if unfavorable outcomes materialize. Reward can be defined as upside potential, representing the scale of gain that may occur under favorable conditions. When these are evaluated symmetrically, the analysis assumes that a given level of reward can offset a corresponding level of risk. In practice, this relationship is distorted by asymmetry.

Perceived balance often ignores tail risk. Tail risk refers to outcomes that lie at the extremes of the distribution, particularly those with low probability but high impact. These outcomes are not prominent in average-based evaluations because they occur infrequently. However, their impact is substantial when they do occur. The system is exposed to these outcomes regardless of their probability, and their presence defines the true structure of risk.

High-frequency gains can mask large embedded losses. When a decision produces consistent positive outcomes across many instances, the system's evaluation becomes anchored to these results. The presence of a large potential loss may not be immediately visible because it does not manifest under normal conditions. The system interprets the repeated gains as evidence of stability, while the underlying exposure remains untested.

Imbalance emerges when downside exceeds recoverable capacity. Recoverable capacity refers to the system's ability to absorb loss and return to its prior state through subsequent gains. If the magnitude of a potential loss exceeds this capacity, the system cannot recover through normal operation. The loss introduces a structural change that persists, altering the system's trajectory. This imbalance defines a condition where risk is not offset by reward, even if the frequency of gains is higher.

Reward does not offset loss symmetrically because gains and losses interact differently with the system's structure. Gains increase capacity, but they do so incrementally. Losses reduce capacity, and may do so in a way that introduces new constraints or removes existing flexibility. The system's response to these changes is nonlinear. A series of gains may build capacity gradually, while a single loss may remove a significant portion of that capacity at once.

Hidden downside emerges when exposure to loss is not visible under normal conditions. This exposure exists within the payoff structure but does not manifest until specific conditions are met. The system may operate for extended periods without encountering these conditions, creating the impression that the decision carries limited risk. This impression is conditional on the absence of triggering events.

Certain risks are latent, meaning they are embedded within the system but not actively influencing outcomes until activated. These risks may be associated with specific thresholds, external shocks, or combinations of variables that occur infrequently. The system's evaluation of the decision is therefore based on a subset of its possible outcomes, excluding those that have not yet been realized.

Stability in normal conditions conceals asymmetry. When the system experiences a sequence of favorable or neutral outcomes, the absence of visible loss reinforces the perception that the decision structure is balanced. The system's exposure to extreme outcomes remains present, but it is not observable within the current state. This concealment is structural. It arises from the distribution of outcomes, where significant losses are positioned at the edges rather than within the central range.

Hidden downside becomes visible under stress. Stress introduces conditions that increase the likelihood of extreme outcomes or activate latent risks. When these conditions occur, the system experiences outcomes that were previously outside its observed range. The structural asymmetry becomes apparent as the system responds to losses that exceed its prior experience. This transition often appears abrupt because the system moves from a state of apparent stability to one of significant disruption.

The absence of loss does not imply the absence of exposure. A system may operate without experiencing negative outcomes for an extended period, yet still carry significant downside risk. The evaluation of stability based solely on observed outcomes is therefore incomplete. It reflects the system's recent experience, not the full range of its potential states. Exposure exists independently of whether it has been realized.

Payoff structure, risk-reward imbalance, and hidden downside together define how decisions influence system trajectory. The distribution of outcomes determines the system's exposure to extreme events, while asymmetry defines how those events interact with capacity and constraints. Hidden downside ensures that this exposure is not always visible, particularly under stable conditions. These elements combine to create a decision environment where structural impact is determined by tail outcomes rather than average results.

Symmetric evaluation fails under asymmetric conditions because it treats gains and losses as interchangeable. It assumes that the accumulation of positive outcomes can offset negative ones in a linear manner. In asymmetric systems, this assumption breaks down. The impact of a large loss cannot be neutralized by a series of smaller gains if the loss alters the system's structure. Evaluation that does not account for this asymmetry misrepresents the decision's effect on the system.

Decisions must therefore be understood through downside exposure. Downside exposure represents the portion of the payoff structure associated with negative outcomes, particularly those with large magnitude. This exposure defines the system's vulnerability to disruption. The system's trajectory is influenced more by these potential losses than by the frequency of gains, because losses have the capacity to alter the system in ways that gains do not.

Asymmetrical evaluation involves weighting outcomes based on their structural impact rather than their frequency. This approach recognizes that not all outcomes contribute equally to the system's trajectory. High-impact events, even if rare, carry greater significance than low-impact events that occur frequently. The system's behavior over time reflects the influence of these high-impact events, as they define the boundaries within which the system can operate.

Systems are shaped by tail events, not by averages. The average outcome represents a central tendency that may never actually occur in practice. The system experiences discrete events drawn from the distribution, including those at its extremes. When an extreme event occurs, its impact is immediate and persistent. It redefines the system's state, influencing all subsequent decisions and outcomes.

The Decision Asymmetry Mechanism establishes that the structural importance of a decision lies in its payoff distribution. Decisions are not equivalent based on their expected outcomes alone. They differ based on how gains and losses are distributed, how these outcomes interact with system capacity, and how exposure to extreme events is embedded within the structure. The system's stability is determined by how it responds to these distributions, particularly to the presence of large negative outcomes.

As decisions accumulate, the system's exposure to asymmetric payoffs becomes a defining characteristic of its trajectory. Each decision contributes to the overall distribution of possible outcomes, shaping the system's sensitivity to loss and its capacity to absorb it. The interaction between these decisions determines whether the system remains within its tolerance range or moves toward instability.

Understanding asymmetry reframes how decisions are interpreted within a financial system. It shifts the focus from frequency to impact, from averages to distributions, and from visible outcomes to embedded exposure. The system does not evolve based on typical conditions. It evolves based on how it responds to the full range of possible outcomes, including those that occur infrequently but carry significant structural weight.

As the system continues to operate under uncertainty, the presence of asymmetric payoff structures defines its vulnerability to disruption. Decisions that appear stable under normal conditions may carry hidden exposure that becomes visible only under stress. The system's trajectory is therefore influenced not only by what is observed, but by what remains latent within the distribution of outcomes.

The Time Horizon Mechanism

Time is not a neutral dimension within a financial system. It alters how decisions are evaluated, how outcomes are observed, and how the system's trajectory is interpreted. A decision does not produce a single, immediate effect. It generates a sequence of effects distributed across time, some visible in the near term and others emerging only after extended intervals. The system interacts with these effects unevenly, because visibility, feedback, and constraint vary across time horizons. This variation creates structural distortions in how decisions are understood and how they influence stability.

Short-term bias arises from the prioritization of immediate outcomes over those that occur later. This bias is not introduced as a preference in isolation. It emerges from the structure of the decision environment, where near-term outcomes are observable, measurable, and directly connected to recent actions. The system receives rapid feedback from short-term results, allowing it to interpret decisions in close temporal proximity to their execution. This proximity creates a strong linkage between action and outcome, reinforcing the importance of the short term within the evaluation process.

Decision environments emphasize near-term visibility because the system's monitoring capacity is aligned with immediate states. Financial flows, obligations, and operational conditions are tracked in real time or near real time. These elements produce continuous signals that the system can observe and respond to. Long-term outcomes, by contrast, are not directly visible. They are inferred through projections or delayed observations, which carry greater uncertainty. The system therefore anchors its evaluation to what can be seen with clarity, which is the short-term result.

Short-term outcomes dominate evaluation because they provide direct feedback. The system can associate a decision with an observable result within a relatively short interval, allowing it to form a judgment about the effectiveness of that decision. This feedback loop is structurally reinforced by the frequency of observation. Decisions are made continuously, and outcomes are assessed in the same continuous framework. The system becomes conditioned to evaluate decisions based on the outcomes that appear within this immediate cycle.

Immediate feedback distorts perceived decision quality by compressing the evaluation window. When a decision produces a favorable short-term outcome, it is interpreted as aligned with system objectives, regardless of its long-term implications. Conversely, an unfavorable short-term outcome may be interpreted as misalignment, even if the decision introduces benefits that materialize over a longer horizon. The system's perception of quality is therefore tied to timing rather than to the full distribution of outcomes.

This distortion shifts the system's trajectory incrementally. Each decision is evaluated based on its short-term result, and subsequent decisions are influenced by this evaluation. Over time, the system begins to favor decisions that produce immediate positive feedback, even if those decisions introduce latent risks or long-term instability. The trajectory changes not through a single large adjustment, but through the accumulation of many small directional shifts aligned with short-term outcomes.

Delayed consequences represent the portion of a decision's effects that do not materialize within the immediate evaluation window. These consequences may arise from structural changes introduced by the decision, interactions between variables that unfold over time, or external conditions that evolve after the decision has been made. The system does not observe these consequences at the moment of decision. They emerge later, often after multiple subsequent decisions have already been made.

A decision can therefore appear stable in the short term while introducing instability in the long term. The system may experience a sequence of favorable or neutral outcomes immediately following the decision, reinforcing the perception that the decision is aligned with its structure. During this period, the delayed effects remain unobserved. When they eventually materialize, they may alter the system's configuration in ways that were not anticipated during the initial evaluation.

Structural effects are often not visible immediately because they require time to propagate through the system. A change introduced at one point may influence other components only after certain thresholds are reached or after interactions accumulate. This propagation creates a temporal gap between cause and effect. The system experiences the cause at one point in time and the effect at another, with no direct visibility into the connection during the intervening period.

Delay creates separation between cause and effect, weakening the system's ability to link decisions to outcomes accurately. When an outcome appears long after the decision that contributed to it, the system may not associate the two. Subsequent decisions may have been made under different conditions, further obscuring the connection. The evaluation process becomes fragmented, as the system interprets outcomes based on their timing rather than their origin.

Delayed outcomes accumulate before becoming visible. Multiple decisions may introduce incremental structural changes that do not produce immediate effects. These changes build over time, interacting with each other and with evolving conditions. When the combined effect reaches a threshold, the system experiences a noticeable shift. This shift appears sudden, but it is the result of accumulated delayed consequences that were not visible individually.

Discounting modifies how the system weights outcomes across time horizons. Discounting refers to the reduction in perceived importance of outcomes that occur further in the future relative to those that occur in the present. This reduction is not necessarily explicit. It emerges from the system's interaction with visibility, uncertainty, and feedback. Immediate outcomes are observed directly, while future outcomes are uncertain and require projection. The system therefore assigns greater weight to the outcomes it can observe with clarity.

Systems implicitly reduce the weight of long-term consequences because those consequences are less certain and less directly connected to current decisions. The evaluation process relies on available information, and information about future states is inherently incomplete. As a result, the system prioritizes outcomes that can be measured and verified in the present. This prioritization reduces the influence of long-term effects within the decision process.

Discounting alters the evaluation of tradeoffs by changing how different outcomes are compared. When a decision involves both immediate and delayed effects, the system evaluates these effects with unequal weight. Immediate outcomes are given greater importance, while delayed outcomes are reduced in significance. This imbalance affects how decisions are selected, as the system favors options that provide short-term benefits even if they introduce long-term costs.

Distant risks are systematically underweighted within this framework. Risks that are expected to materialize in the future are perceived as less critical than those that affect the present. This perception is not based on the magnitude of the risk, but on its temporal position. A large risk that lies outside the immediate horizon may be given less consideration than a smaller risk that is imminent. The system's sensitivity to risk is therefore shaped by time, not solely by magnitude.

Discounting is structural, not purely behavioral. It arises from the system's configuration, including how information is observed, how feedback is received, and how decisions are sequenced. The system does not have equal access to outcomes across all time horizons. It interacts more directly with the present than with the future. This asymmetry in access creates a corresponding asymmetry in evaluation. The system weights outcomes according to their visibility and immediacy.

Short-term bias, delayed consequences, and discounting interact to produce time distortion. Time distortion refers to the misalignment between how outcomes are weighted and how they actually affect the system's trajectory. The system overemphasizes immediate outcomes, underemphasizes delayed consequences, and reduces the perceived importance of future risks. This misweighting alters the decision process, leading to choices that may appear aligned in the short term but introduce instability over longer horizons.

Misalignment across time horizons introduces structural drift. Decisions that are optimized for immediate outcomes may gradually shift the system into configurations that are less stable over time. Each decision contributes a small adjustment to the trajectory, and these adjustments accumulate. The system does not experience this drift as a single event. It unfolds incrementally, as the effects of short-term prioritization compound across multiple decision cycles.

Decisions optimized for the short term may degrade long-term stability because they do not fully account for delayed consequences. The system selects options that produce immediate positive feedback, reinforcing this pattern of selection. Over time, the accumulation of these decisions can reduce capacity, increase exposure, or alter constraints in ways that are not immediately visible. When the delayed effects materialize, the system may find itself in a configuration that is more sensitive to variability and less able to absorb disturbance.

Time distortion is therefore not an isolated phenomenon. It is a continuous condition that shapes how decisions are evaluated and how the system evolves. The system operates across multiple time horizons simultaneously, but its evaluation process is weighted toward the near term. This imbalance affects how decisions are made, how outcomes are interpreted, and how trajectory is adjusted.

Instability emerges gradually through this accumulation of misalignment. The system may appear stable within each short-term interval, as decisions produce favorable or neutral outcomes within that window. However, the underlying trajectory may be shifting toward a less stable configuration. When delayed consequences converge or when external conditions change, the system may experience a transition that reflects the cumulative effect of prior decisions.

The Time Horizon Mechanism establishes that decisions cannot be evaluated independently of their temporal distribution. The system's behavior is shaped not only by what decisions produce, but by when those effects occur and how they are weighted. Short-term bias directs attention toward immediate outcomes, delayed consequences separate cause from effect, and discounting reduces the perceived importance of future states. Together, these factors create a condition in which the system's evaluation process is misaligned with the full temporal structure of its decisions.

As decisions continue to accumulate, the interaction between time horizons defines the system's trajectory. Immediate outcomes influence perception and subsequent choices, while delayed effects alter the system's structure in ways that may not be immediately recognized. The balance between these forces determines whether the system maintains stability or drifts toward instability. Time is therefore not simply a dimension through which decisions pass. It is a structural factor that shapes how decisions are made, evaluated, and integrated into the system over time.

The Scarcity Pressure Mechanism

Scarcity alters the structure of a financial system by compressing the conditions under which decisions are made. It does not simply reduce the quantity of available resources. It changes how the system operates, how decisions are generated, and how outcomes are absorbed. When resources are abundant, the system can extend time horizons, maintain multiple options, and absorb variation without immediate consequence. When resources are constrained, these properties contract simultaneously. The system is forced to operate within narrower limits, and this contraction reshapes the decision environment.

Liquidity represents the system's available capacity to meet obligations and absorb variability. It is not limited to cash balances, but includes all resources that can be mobilized to sustain operations across time. Liquidity defines how long the system can continue functioning without requiring immediate adjustment. When liquidity is sufficient, the system retains temporal flexibility. It can delay decisions, evaluate alternatives, and absorb short-term misalignment without structural disruption.

Reduced liquidity limits this flexibility. As liquidity declines, the system's ability to absorb variability diminishes. Obligations remain constant or increase relative to available capacity, and the margin between current state and constraint narrows. The system becomes more sensitive to timing mismatches and unexpected fluctuations. Decisions that might otherwise be deferred must be addressed within shorter intervals because the system cannot sustain its position without immediate action.

Low liquidity compresses decision timelines. Time is no longer an adjustable variable. The system cannot extend evaluation to incorporate additional information or to consider alternative paths. Instead, it must operate within fixed or shrinking windows defined by its remaining capacity. This compression alters the decision process by reducing the duration available for analysis and increasing the urgency of execution. The system moves from a state where time can be allocated to evaluation to one where time is consumed by necessity.

Liquidity determines buffer capacity against error. When the system has sufficient liquidity, it can absorb the effects of decisions that produce misalignment. Errors can be corrected over time, and the system can adjust its trajectory without immediate structural impact. When liquidity is constrained, this buffer is reduced or eliminated. The system cannot tolerate deviations without consequence. A decision that introduces misalignment may directly affect the system's ability to meet obligations or maintain stability.

Constrained liquidity increases exposure to misalignment because it removes the system's ability to absorb error without disruption. The same decision produces different effects depending on the level of liquidity. In a system with capacity, misalignment may be contained within the buffer. In a system without capacity, misalignment may propagate immediately into instability. Exposure is therefore not only a function of decision structure, but of the system's available capacity to absorb its consequences.

Scarcity introduces forced decisions. A forced decision is one that must be executed without the option to delay, defer, or gather additional information. It arises when the system's constraints eliminate the possibility of waiting. Obligations, deadlines, and resource limitations create conditions where inaction is not neutral. The system must act to maintain continuity, even if the conditions for evaluation are incomplete or unfavorable.

Scarcity removes optionality in timing. Under conditions of sufficient capacity, the system can choose when to act. It can align decisions with favorable conditions, extend evaluation periods, or sequence actions to improve alignment. Under scarcity, this temporal optionality is removed. The system must act within externally or internally imposed timeframes, regardless of whether those timeframes align with optimal evaluation conditions.

Decisions under scarcity are therefore executed under unfavorable conditions. Unfavorable conditions refer to environments where information is incomplete, time is limited, and the system's capacity to absorb error is reduced. The system does not select these conditions. It operates within them because the absence of resources constrains its alternatives. The decision process becomes reactive, oriented toward maintaining function rather than optimizing alignment.

Forced decisions reduce evaluation quality because they limit the system's ability to process information and consider alternatives. Evaluation requires time, capacity, and optionality. When these elements are constrained, the system cannot fully assess the implications of its actions. It proceeds with partial analysis, relying on the information and capacity available within the compressed timeframe. The resulting decision is structurally simplified, reflecting the limitations of the environment rather than the full complexity of the system.

Compulsion replaces selection under scarcity. Selection implies the ability to choose among multiple alternatives based on evaluation. Compulsion implies that the range of alternatives is restricted to those that satisfy immediate constraints. The system is not choosing the best option among many. It is selecting from a limited set of viable actions that prevent immediate failure. This shift changes the nature of decision-making from evaluative to constrained execution.

Option sets define the range of feasible decisions available to the system at any point in time. These sets are determined by the system's current configuration, including its resources, constraints, and exposure. When resources are abundant, option sets are broader. The system can consider multiple paths, each with different tradeoffs and implications. When resources are scarce, option sets contract. Certain paths become inaccessible because they require resources that are no longer available.

Scarcity reduces the number of viable alternatives. Options that depend on time, liquidity, or capacity are removed from the decision space. The system cannot pursue these paths because it lacks the resources to support them. The remaining options are those that can be executed within the current constraints, regardless of their alignment with long-term objectives. This contraction is structural. It reflects the system's reduced ability to maintain multiple potential trajectories.

Reduced options limit the system's ability to select aligned paths. Alignment requires the ability to compare alternatives and choose the one that best fits the system's structure and objectives. When the option set is narrow, this comparison is constrained. The system may be forced to choose an option that is only partially aligned or that introduces new risks, because more suitable alternatives are not available within the constrained set.

Constrained option sets increase the probability of suboptimal outcomes. Suboptimal does not imply incorrect in an absolute sense. It refers to outcomes that are less aligned with the system's structural requirements than alternatives that would have been available under less constrained conditions. The system's ability to achieve alignment is reduced because it cannot access the full range of possible decisions. The resulting trajectory reflects these limitations.

Decision quality declines as choice sets narrow because evaluation is performed over a reduced set of alternatives. Quality is not solely a function of the decision process. It is also a function of the available options.

Even a consistent process cannot produce highly aligned outcomes if the option set is constrained to choices that do not fully meet the system's requirements. The system's decisions are therefore shaped by the structure of the option set as much as by the evaluation applied to it.

Liquidity constraints, forced decisions, and narrow option sets operate together to define the Scarcity Pressure Mechanism. Each element contributes to the compression of the decision environment. Liquidity constraints reduce the system's capacity to absorb variability, forced decisions eliminate temporal optionality, and narrow option sets limit the range of feasible actions. These factors are not independent. They reinforce each other, creating a compounded effect on decision-making.

Scarcity increases both the frequency and magnitude of error. Frequency increases because decisions are made more often under constrained conditions, where evaluation is limited and option sets are narrow. Magnitude increases because the system's reduced capacity amplifies the impact of misalignment. Errors that would have been absorbed under conditions of abundance propagate more directly into structural consequences under scarcity.

Mistakes under scarcity have amplified structural impact because the system lacks the buffers required to contain them. A decision that introduces misalignment may immediately affect the system's ability to meet obligations or maintain stability. The absence of capacity means that the system cannot isolate the effect of the error. It becomes integrated into the system's trajectory, influencing subsequent decisions and outcomes.

Scarcity pressure functions as a multiplier on existing system weaknesses. Weaknesses that are latent under conditions of abundance become active under constraint. A system that appears stable when resources are sufficient may reveal fragility when those resources are reduced. The same structural configuration produces different outcomes depending on the level of scarcity, because scarcity exposes the system's sensitivity to constraint.

As scarcity increases, the system becomes more fragile. Fragility is defined by the system's sensitivity to disturbance and its reduced ability to absorb error. Under scarcity, small deviations can produce significant effects because the system operates close to its limits. The margin for error is minimal, and the capacity for correction is constrained. The system's stability is therefore dependent on its ability to function within these compressed conditions.

Scarcity is not a temporary condition that can be isolated from the system's structure. It is a state that interacts with all aspects of decision-making, altering how decisions are generated, evaluated, and applied. The system does not simply operate with fewer resources. It operates differently. The mechanisms that govern decision-making are modified by the presence of constraint, producing outcomes that reflect the compressed environment.

As decisions accumulate under scarcity, their effects compound. Each decision is made within a constrained environment, contributing to the system's trajectory. The accumulation of these decisions reflects the limitations of the conditions under which they were made. The system's evolution is therefore shaped not only by the decisions themselves, but by the environment that produced them.

The Scarcity Pressure Mechanism establishes that resource availability is not merely a background condition. It is a defining factor in how decisions function within a financial system. When resources are constrained, the system's decision environment is compressed, increasing the likelihood of misalignment and amplifying the impact of error. Stability under these conditions depends on how the system absorbs and responds to the structural changes introduced by scarcity.

The Margin Stability Mechanism

Margin defines the distance between a system's current capacity and the demands placed upon it. It represents excess capacity relative to obligations, not as an incidental surplus but as a structural condition that shapes how the system operates. When margin is present, the system is not positioned directly against its constraints. It occupies a range within which variation can occur without immediately triggering pressure. This positioning alters the environment in which decisions are made, changing how time, options, and evaluation interact.

Buffers are the operational expression of margin. They are the resources—liquidity, time, and flexible capacity—that absorb variability and error without forcing immediate adjustment. A buffer does not eliminate disturbance. It intercepts its impact, preventing it from propagating directly into system instability. When a system contains buffers, outcomes that deviate from expectation are contained within the margin rather than transmitted into constraint boundaries.

Margin creates separation between system state and constraint thresholds. This separation is not merely spatial or conceptual. It defines the system's tolerance range. When the system is positioned away from its limits, disturbances can occur without altering its structural configuration. The system remains within its operational envelope, even as conditions fluctuate. When margin is absent, this separation collapses. Any deviation brings the system into direct contact with its constraints, converting variability into pressure.

Buffers reduce sensitivity to disturbance by absorbing the initial impact of misalignment. Sensitivity refers to how strongly the system reacts to deviations from expected conditions. In a buffered system, small or moderate disturbances are dampened. They do not produce immediate structural change because the buffer absorbs the discrepancy between expectation and reality. In an unbuffered system, the same disturbance produces a direct effect, as there is no intermediary capacity to contain it.

Margin increases tolerance for misalignment by allowing the system to operate with imperfect decisions without immediate consequence. Misalignment is inevitable, as decisions are made under constraint, uncertainty, and incomplete information. When margin exists, the system can accommodate these imperfections. The effects of misalignment are distributed over time, allowing the system to adjust gradually rather than abruptly. When margin is absent, misalignment translates directly into pressure, forcing immediate corrective action.

Buffer depth determines the stability range of the system. Depth refers to the extent of excess capacity relative to obligations. A shallow buffer provides limited absorption, allowing only minor deviations to be contained. A deeper buffer extends the range of variability the system can withstand without structural change. The system's stability is therefore not defined by the absence of disturbance, but by the depth of its buffers relative to the magnitude of potential deviations.

Urgency emerges when the system approaches its constraints. It is the compression of time that occurs when decisions must be made within narrow intervals to prevent immediate consequence. Urgency is not an inherent property of decisions. It is a function of the system's position relative to its limits. When margin is present, urgency is reduced because the system is not required to act immediately to maintain stability.

Margin extends available decision timelines by decoupling action from immediate necessity. When the system has capacity beyond its obligations, it can delay decisions without incurring immediate cost. This extension of time alters the decision environment. Evaluation can proceed over longer intervals, allowing additional information to be incorporated and alternative paths to be considered. The system is not forced to act at the earliest possible moment. It can align decision timing with conditions rather than with constraint.

Reduced urgency allows deeper evaluation. Depth in evaluation requires time to process information, assess interactions, and consider multiple outcomes. When urgency is high, this depth is truncated. The system prioritizes immediacy over completeness. When urgency is reduced through margin, the system can sustain more comprehensive evaluation. It can examine the structure of decisions rather than relying on simplified representations necessitated by time compression.

Margin decouples decision timing from immediate constraint. In a constrained system, decisions are synchronized with obligations and deadlines. The system must act in response to external or internal demands, often under unfavorable conditions. With margin, this synchronization is loosened. Decisions can be sequenced independently of immediate pressures, allowing the system to select timing that improves alignment with its structure and environment.

Urgency decreases as capacity increases because the system's need to act immediately is reduced. This relationship is not linear. Small increases in capacity may produce modest reductions in urgency, while larger increases can significantly expand the decision window. The system's behavior shifts as this relationship changes. With greater capacity, the system transitions from reactive timing to flexible timing, altering how decisions are generated and applied.

Option sets define the range of feasible decisions available to the system at any given point. These sets are determined by the system's resources, constraints, and current configuration. When margin is present, option sets expand. The system can access a broader range of paths because it has the capacity to support them. When margin is absent, option sets contract, limiting the system to decisions that satisfy immediate constraints.

Margin increases the number of viable alternatives by enabling the system to consider paths that require time, resources, or flexibility. These paths may not be accessible under constrained conditions because they depend on the system's ability to absorb interim variability. With margin, the system can sustain these paths long enough to realize their potential outcomes. The expansion of viable alternatives is therefore a direct function of available capacity.

Additional capacity enables access to more paths by removing constraints that would otherwise eliminate them from consideration. A decision path that requires delayed payoff, staged execution, or tolerance for short-term misalignment becomes feasible when the system has sufficient margin. Without margin, such paths are excluded from the decision space because the system cannot sustain the conditions they require.

Expanded option sets improve alignment potential by increasing the probability that a decision can match the system's structural requirements. Alignment depends on the availability of alternatives that fit the system's constraints, exposures, and objectives. When the option set is broad, the system can select from a range of possibilities, increasing the likelihood of finding a path that maintains stability. When the option set is narrow, alignment is constrained by the limited alternatives available.

Optionality is a function of available capacity. It is not an abstract property independent of the system's resources. The ability to maintain multiple potential trajectories depends on the system's capacity to support them. Margin provides this capacity, allowing the system to hold multiple options simultaneously or to transition between them without immediate cost. Without margin, optionality collapses, and the system is confined to a restricted set of paths.

Buffers, reduced urgency, and expanded option sets interact to define the Margin Stability Mechanism. Each component modifies the decision environment in a way that increases the system's ability to operate without compression. Buffers absorb variability, reducing the immediate impact of misalignment. Reduced urgency extends decision timelines, allowing deeper evaluation. Expanded option sets increase the range of feasible decisions, improving alignment potential. Together, these factors transform how decisions are generated and applied.

Margin improves both the frequency and quality of decisions by altering the conditions under which they occur. Frequency is affected because the system is not forced into reactive decision cycles driven by constraint. Decisions can be spaced and sequenced more deliberately. Quality is affected because evaluation can incorporate more information and consider a broader range of alternatives. The system is not constrained to simplified decision structures imposed by time and resource limitations.

Capacity expansion reduces error propagation by containing the effects of misalignment within buffers. When an error occurs, it does not immediately translate into structural disruption. The system can absorb the discrepancy and adjust over time. This containment prevents errors from cascading through subsequent decisions, reducing their cumulative impact on the system's trajectory.

Stability can be defined as the system's ability to operate without compression. Compression occurs when constraints, limited resources, and urgency converge to restrict the decision environment. A stable system maintains sufficient margin to avoid this convergence. It operates within a range where decisions can be made without immediate pressure, allowing the system to maintain coherence across time.

Margin transforms the decision environment from reactive to flexible. In a reactive environment, decisions are driven by immediate constraints and executed under compressed conditions. In a flexible environment, decisions are shaped by the system's structure and evaluated within extended timeframes. This transformation does not eliminate uncertainty or variability. It changes how the system interacts with them, allowing for adjustment and absorption rather than immediate reaction.

As the system evolves, the presence or absence of margin determines how it responds to changing conditions. When margin is maintained, the system retains its ability to absorb disturbance and adapt its trajectory. When margin is eroded, the system moves toward a state where decisions are made under increasing pressure, reducing evaluation quality and increasing exposure to error. The trajectory is therefore influenced not only by the decisions themselves, but by the capacity within which those decisions are made.

The Margin Stability Mechanism establishes that excess capacity is not passive. It actively shapes the decision environment, influencing time, optionality, and evaluation depth. Margin is not merely surplus that remains unused. It is the structural condition that allows the system to operate without immediate constraint, maintaining stability across varying conditions.

The Volatility Exposure Mechanism

Volatility alters the structure of a financial system by introducing variability into the inputs that decisions depend on. It is not limited to the presence of uncertainty. It is the continuous fluctuation of conditions—timing, magnitude, and sequencing—that prevents the system from stabilizing around a consistent baseline. Decisions are not made against fixed parameters. They are made against inputs that change between decision cycles, altering both the information available and the conditions under which that information must be interpreted.

Irregular income represents one of the primary channels through which volatility enters the system. Income is not only a measure of magnitude. It is a sequence of inflows distributed across time. When income is regular, both in timing and amount, the system can anchor its operations to a predictable cycle. Obligations can be sequenced relative to inflows, and decision timing can align with known resource availability. When income becomes irregular, this anchoring is disrupted.

Irregular income is defined by variability in both the timing and magnitude of inflows. Payments may arrive at inconsistent intervals, and the amounts may vary across those intervals. This variability introduces uncertainty into the system's resource availability at any given point. The system cannot rely on a fixed schedule or predictable quantity of inflow to guide its decisions. Each decision must account for the possibility that future inflows may not align with past patterns.

Inconsistent inflows disrupt planning cycles by breaking the synchronization between resource availability and obligation timing. Planning cycles depend on the ability to align expected inflows with expected outflows. When inflows are irregular, this alignment cannot be maintained with precision. The system may experience periods of surplus followed by periods of constraint, even if the total inflow over time remains constant. The distribution of income across time becomes as significant as its aggregate amount.

Income variability alters system timing and sequencing. Decisions are not made in isolation. They are sequenced relative to prior and subsequent actions, with timing playing a critical role in how outcomes propagate through the system. When income timing is inconsistent, the sequencing of decisions must adapt continuously. Actions that depend on future inflows cannot be scheduled with certainty, and the system must adjust its sequence in response to each new inflow event.

Predictable inflow stabilizes the decision environment because it provides a consistent reference point for timing and magnitude. When inflows are known in advance, the system can align its decisions with these expectations. Evaluation can incorporate stable assumptions about resource availability, and the system can maintain coherence across decision cycles. Predictability does not eliminate variability in outcomes, but it reduces variability in inputs, allowing the system to operate with a stable baseline.

Irregular income increases uncertainty in resource availability by removing this baseline. The system must operate with incomplete knowledge of when and how much resource will be available in future periods. This uncertainty affects not only individual decisions but the structure of the decision process itself. The system cannot rely on fixed assumptions and must continuously adjust to new information as it becomes available.

Variable conditions extend beyond income to include both external and internal factors that influence the system's operation. External conditions may include market environments, economic shifts, or changes in external demand. Internal conditions may include fluctuations in expenses, changes in obligations, or shifts in capacity. These conditions do not remain constant. They evolve over time, often in ways that are not fully predictable at the moment of decision.

Variable conditions are defined by their fluctuation across time and across states. They do not follow a fixed pattern that can be reliably projected. Instead, they introduce dispersion into the inputs that the system must evaluate. Each decision is made under a slightly different configuration of conditions, even if the underlying structure of the system remains the same. This variability alters how decisions are interpreted and how outcomes are produced.

Changing conditions alter decision inputs by modifying the information available for evaluation. Inputs that were valid in one period may no longer apply in the next. Assumptions based on prior states may not hold under new conditions. The system must continuously update its evaluation framework to account for these changes, but it does so under constraint, with limited time and incomplete information.

Instability in inputs reduces consistency of evaluation. Consistency requires that decisions be evaluated under similar conditions across time. When inputs fluctuate, the basis for comparison changes. The system cannot apply the same evaluation process with the same inputs across different decision cycles. This leads to variation in how decisions are assessed, even if the underlying process remains unchanged.

Variability introduces dispersion in outcomes. When inputs fluctuate, the range of possible outcomes expands. The system experiences a wider distribution of results, reflecting the variability in the conditions under which decisions are made. This dispersion is not solely a function of decision quality. It is a reflection of the environment in which the system operates. Even consistent processes can produce variable outcomes when inputs are unstable.

Systems operating under variable conditions do not have stable baseline states. A baseline represents a reference condition against which deviations can be measured. When conditions are stable, the system can identify what constitutes normal operation and what constitutes deviation. Under variability, this baseline shifts continuously. The system must operate without a fixed point of reference, making it more difficult to distinguish between expected variation and structural change.

Planning is the process of projecting decisions across time, linking current actions to future outcomes. It relies on the ability to estimate future states with sufficient accuracy to guide present decisions. Planning does not require certainty, but it requires a degree of predictability that allows the system to form coherent expectations about future conditions. When volatility is present, this predictability is reduced.

Volatility reduces the reliability of projections by increasing the range of possible future states. The system cannot assume that current conditions will persist or that past patterns will continue. Projections must account for a wider set of potential scenarios, each with different implications for the system's trajectory. This expansion of possible states reduces the precision of any single projection.

Future states become less predictable under variability because the inputs that determine those states are themselves unstable. Income may fluctuate, expenses may vary, and external conditions may shift in ways that are not fully captured by existing models. The system must therefore operate with projections that are inherently uncertain, reflecting a range of possible outcomes rather than a single expected path.

Planning becomes probabilistic rather than deterministic under these conditions. Deterministic planning assumes that a given set of actions will lead to a predictable outcome. Probabilistic planning acknowledges that multiple outcomes are possible, each with a certain likelihood. The system does not project a single future state, but a distribution of potential states. Decisions are made with reference to this distribution rather than to a fixed expectation.

Unstable inputs reduce the effectiveness of long-term alignment because they undermine the connection between current decisions and future outcomes. Alignment requires that decisions be coordinated across time, with each action contributing to a coherent trajectory. When inputs are volatile, this coordination becomes more difficult. The system cannot reliably link present actions to future states, as the conditions that will influence those states are uncertain.

Irregular income, variable conditions, and planning difficulty interact to define the Volatility Exposure Mechanism. Each component contributes to the reduction of predictability within the system. Irregular income disrupts timing and resource availability, variable conditions alter decision inputs, and planning difficulty reduces the reliability of projections. Together, these factors create an environment where the system operates without stable reference points.

Volatility reduces the system's ability to forecast and align decisions because it introduces variability into both inputs and outcomes. Forecasting depends on the ability to project future states with some degree of accuracy. When inputs are unstable, these projections become less reliable. Alignment depends on the ability to sequence decisions across time in a coherent manner. When conditions change between decision cycles, this sequencing is disrupted.

Predictability is required for stable sequencing because it allows the system to coordinate decisions across time. When predictability is present, the system can align actions with expected conditions, maintaining coherence in its trajectory. When predictability is reduced, this alignment becomes fragmented. Decisions are made in response to current conditions without a stable link to future states, leading to dispersion in outcomes.

Volatility exposure can be defined as the system's sensitivity to fluctuating inputs. A system with high exposure experiences significant variation in its inputs, leading to greater dispersion in outcomes and reduced predictability. This exposure is structural. It arises from the nature of the inputs themselves, not from the decisions made within the system. The system's response to volatility depends on how it is configured to absorb or adapt to these fluctuations.

Reduced predictability increases decision error and instability. Error increases because decisions are made with less reliable information about future conditions. Instability increases because the system cannot maintain consistent alignment across time. Each decision is made under a different set of conditions, and the cumulative effect of these decisions reflects the variability of the environment.

The Volatility Exposure Mechanism establishes that variability is not a peripheral factor in decision-making. It is a central condition that shapes how decisions are evaluated and executed. The system does not operate in a stable environment with occasional disturbances. It operates within a continuously fluctuating context, where inputs, timing, and conditions are in motion.

As decisions accumulate under volatility, their effects compound across a range of possible states. The system's trajectory reflects not a single path, but the interaction between decisions and the variability of the environment. Stability is not defined by the elimination of volatility, but by how the system functions within it.

The Complexity Overload Mechanism

A financial system operates by interpreting inputs, evaluating relationships, and producing decisions that alter its trajectory. This process depends on the system's capacity to process information coherently. Capacity is not unlimited. It is defined by the system's ability to integrate variables, assess interactions, and maintain consistency across evaluation cycles. As the number of inputs increases, the system approaches a point where the volume and complexity of information exceed this capacity. At that point, the structure of decision-making changes.

Cognitive capacity can be defined as the system's ability to process information and evaluate decisions within the constraints of time, attention, and structural bandwidth. It determines how many variables can be considered simultaneously, how deeply interactions can be analyzed, and how consistently evaluation can be applied across different decision instances. This capacity is finite. It does not scale proportionally with the number of inputs available to the system.

As inputs increase, processing limits are reached. Each additional variable introduces not only its own informational content but also potential interactions with other variables. The system must account for these interactions to maintain coherent evaluation. When the number of inputs exceeds the system's ability to process them fully, the evaluation process becomes fragmented. The system cannot maintain a complete representation of all relevant factors simultaneously.

Overload occurs when the volume of information exceeds processing capacity. Under overload, clarity is reduced because the system cannot fully integrate all inputs into a coherent model. Some variables are processed, others are partially processed, and some are excluded entirely. The system's representation of the decision environment becomes incomplete and inconsistent. This inconsistency affects how decisions are generated and applied.

Consistency is also reduced under overload. Consistency requires that the same evaluation process be applied across different decision instances. When the system is overloaded, it cannot sustain this uniformity. Different subsets of variables may be considered in different instances, leading to variation in how decisions are evaluated. The system's outputs become less predictable, not because the environment has changed, but because the evaluation process has become unstable.

Decision simplification emerges as a structural response to overload. Simplification involves reducing the number of variables considered, focusing on a subset of inputs that can be processed within the system's capacity. This reduction is not necessarily deliberate. It is a consequence of the system's inability to process all available information. The system defaults to manageable representations, prioritizing certain variables while excluding others.

Reduced clarity increases the probability of misalignment. Misalignment occurs when the decision does not correspond to the system's actual conditions or structural requirements. When clarity is reduced, the system's representation of those conditions is incomplete. Decisions are made based on partial information, increasing the likelihood that important variables or interactions are not accounted for. The resulting decisions may appear coherent within the simplified model but diverge from the system's full complexity.

The presence of multiple variables defines a multi-variable system. Such a system includes numerous factors that influence outcomes, each interacting with others in ways that are not always linear or independent. Variables may include income streams, expense categories, timing constraints, external conditions, and internal capacities. Each variable contributes to the system's behavior, but its effect is shaped by its interaction with other variables.

Variable interactions increase complexity nonlinearly. When two variables interact, the system must consider their combined effect. As more variables are added, the number of potential interactions increases at a rate that exceeds the growth in the number of variables themselves. This creates a multiplicative effect, where the system's complexity expands faster than its input count. The system must process not only individual variables but the relationships between them.

Outcomes in a multi-variable system depend on these relationships rather than on individual inputs alone. A variable that appears insignificant in isolation may have substantial impact when combined with others. Conversely, a variable that appears significant may have limited effect if its interactions are constrained. The system's behavior emerges from the network of interactions, not from any single input. This makes evaluation more complex, as the system must consider both individual variables and their interdependencies.

More variables increase uncertainty in evaluation because they expand the range of possible outcomes. Each additional variable introduces new potential states, and each interaction between variables creates additional pathways through which outcomes can emerge. The system cannot fully map all these pathways within its processing limits. As a result, evaluation must operate on partial representations, increasing uncertainty about how decisions will translate into outcomes.

System complexity expands faster than processing capacity because the growth in interactions outpaces the system's ability to analyze them. Even if the system increases its processing effort, it cannot fully compensate for the exponential increase in complexity. This divergence creates a structural imbalance, where the system is required to evaluate more information than it can process coherently. The result is a persistent condition of overload.

Signals are the inputs used to guide decision-making. They provide information about the system's state, external conditions, and potential outcomes. Signals can originate from internal metrics, external data, or inferred relationships. The system relies on these signals to form its evaluation and to determine how decisions should be structured.

In complex environments, multiple signals are present simultaneously. These signals may not align. Different inputs may suggest different courses of action, reflecting the variability and interaction within the system. A signal indicating stability in one dimension may coexist with a signal indicating instability in another. The system must interpret these signals collectively, but it may not be able to reconcile them fully.

Conflicting signals arise when inputs provide contradictory information about the system's state or the expected outcomes of a decision. These conflicts are not anomalies. They are inherent in systems where multiple variables interact in complex ways. Each signal reflects a partial perspective, and when combined, these perspectives may not form a coherent whole.

Conflicting inputs reduce confidence and clarity. Confidence depends on the system's ability to form a consistent interpretation of available information. When signals conflict, the system cannot establish a clear direction based on all inputs. It must either resolve the conflict by prioritizing certain signals or operate within the ambiguity created by the contradiction. In either case, clarity is reduced.

The system cannot fully resolve all contradictions because doing so would require complete information and unlimited processing capacity. Resolving conflicts involves assessing the relative importance of signals, understanding their interactions, and predicting how they will influence outcomes. Under conditions of complexity and constraint, this level of resolution is not achievable. The system must operate with unresolved conflicts embedded in its evaluation.

Conflict forces prioritization under uncertainty. When signals cannot be reconciled, the system must select which inputs to emphasize and which to de-emphasize. This prioritization is constrained by the system's capacity and the urgency of the decision. It may not reflect the true structural importance of the signals, but rather their visibility or immediacy. The resulting decision is shaped by how the system resolves—or fails to resolve—these conflicts.

Cognitive overload, multi-variable interaction, and conflicting signals combine to define the Complexity Overload Mechanism. Each element contributes to a condition where the system's processing capacity is exceeded by the demands of the environment. Overload reduces clarity and consistency, multi-variable interaction expands the range of possible outcomes, and conflicting signals introduce ambiguity into evaluation. Together, these factors alter how decisions are produced.

Complexity reduces decision accuracy by increasing the gap between the system's representation of conditions and the actual structure of those conditions. Accuracy depends on the system's ability to incorporate relevant variables and their interactions into its evaluation. When complexity exceeds capacity, this incorporation is incomplete. Decisions are based on simplified models that do not fully capture the system's dynamics.

Error probability increases as complexity exceeds capacity. Error, defined as misalignment between decision and system reality, becomes more likely when the system cannot process all relevant information. The probability of misalignment is not constant. It increases with the degree of overload, as more variables and interactions remain unaccounted for in the decision process.

Overload is a structural condition, not a temporary state. It arises whenever the system's complexity exceeds its processing capacity, regardless of whether this condition persists or fluctuates. Temporary increases in complexity may produce transient overload, while sustained complexity may produce a continuous state of overload. In both cases, the effect on decision-making is structural, altering how decisions are generated and evaluated.

Systems must operate within manageable levels of complexity to maintain coherent decision-making. Manageable complexity does not imply simplicity. It implies that the system's processing capacity is sufficient to integrate the variables and interactions relevant to its decisions. When this balance is maintained, the system can evaluate decisions with greater clarity and consistency. When it is not, the system's evaluation process becomes fragmented.

As complexity increases, the system responds by simplifying, filtering, and structuring its decision process. Simplification reduces the number of variables considered, filtering prioritizes certain signals over others, and structuring imposes frameworks that limit the scope of evaluation. These responses are not optional. They are necessary adaptations to the limits of processing capacity. However, they also introduce their own forms of distortion, as they exclude or de-emphasize certain aspects of the system.

The Complexity Overload Mechanism establishes that complexity is not inherently destabilizing, but becomes so when it exceeds the system's ability to process it coherently. The system's stability depends on the relationship between the complexity of its environment and its capacity to interpret that environment. When this relationship is balanced, decisions can be made with relative accuracy. When it is not, the system operates under conditions of overload, increasing the likelihood of error and misalignment.

The Constraint-Based Decision Mechanism

Constraints are often interpreted as limitations that restrict what a system can do. Within a financial system, this interpretation is incomplete. Constraints do not only reduce the number of possible actions. They shape the decision environment by defining what is feasible, what is acceptable, and what is structurally aligned. In doing so, they alter how decisions are evaluated. Rather than expanding the decision space to include all theoretically possible options, constraints reduce that space to a subset that conforms to the system's requirements. This reduction changes both the complexity of evaluation and the probability of alignment.

A constraint can be defined as a limit on feasible actions imposed by the system's structure, capacity, and exposure. These limits are not arbitrary. They arise from the system's configuration—its obligations, resources, timing requirements, and tolerance for variability. Any decision that violates these limits cannot be sustained without introducing instability. Constraints therefore define the outer boundaries of viable action. Within these boundaries, decisions can be evaluated. Outside them, decisions are structurally misaligned.

Constraint filtering is the process through which these limits remove options that do not conform to system requirements. The system does not evaluate every possible action. It first applies constraints to eliminate those that are incompatible with its structure. This filtering occurs before detailed evaluation. Options that exceed capacity, violate timing constraints, or introduce unacceptable exposure are excluded from consideration. The remaining options form the feasible set.

Filtering reduces the number of decisions that must be evaluated. Without constraints, the system faces an expansive set of possible actions, each requiring assessment. This expansion increases complexity and places greater demands on processing capacity. With constraints, the system operates within a narrower space. Evaluation can be focused on options that are structurally viable, reducing the cognitive and computational load required to assess them.

Fewer options increase clarity because the system can allocate its processing capacity more effectively. When the option set is large, evaluation becomes fragmented, as the system cannot fully process all alternatives. When the option set is reduced through constraint filtering, the system can examine each remaining option with greater depth. The relationships between variables become more visible, and the tradeoffs between options can be assessed with greater precision.

Constraints reduce noise in the decision environment by excluding inputs and options that do not contribute to alignment. Noise refers to information or alternatives that do not materially affect the system's stability but complicate evaluation. When constraints are applied, many of these elements are removed. The system's focus shifts to the variables and options that are relevant within its structural limits. This reduction in noise improves the signal-to-noise ratio within the decision process, enhancing clarity.

Boundaries extend the function of constraints by providing explicit limits within which decisions must operate. While constraints define what is not feasible, boundaries define the permissible range of action. They translate abstract limits into concrete parameters that can be applied consistently across decisions. A boundary may define acceptable levels of exposure, timing intervals, or resource allocation. These boundaries serve as reference points for evaluation.

Boundary-based decisions are evaluated against these explicit limits rather than against an open-ended set of possibilities. The presence of boundaries simplifies evaluation by providing clear criteria for inclusion and exclusion. The system does not need to determine from first principles whether an option is acceptable. It can compare the option against established limits. If the option falls within the boundary, it remains viable. If it falls outside, it is excluded.

Boundaries create consistent evaluation criteria across decision cycles. Consistency requires that similar conditions produce similar evaluations. Without boundaries, the system must interpret each decision in context, potentially applying different criteria in different instances. With boundaries, the criteria are fixed. The system applies the same limits to each decision, regardless of contextual variation. This consistency reduces variability in decision outputs that arises from shifting evaluation standards.

Decisions are simplified when evaluated against fixed constraints because the system does not need to consider the full range of possible outcomes. It can focus on whether the decision satisfies the boundary conditions. This simplification does not eliminate complexity entirely, but it reduces the dimensions that must be considered. The system can operate within a structured framework, where evaluation is guided by predefined limits rather than by open-ended exploration.

Boundaries improve consistency across decision cycles by stabilizing the evaluation process. When the system encounters similar conditions, it applies the same boundaries, leading to similar decisions. This stability reduces the dispersion of outcomes that arises from inconsistent evaluation. The system's trajectory becomes more coherent, as decisions are aligned with a consistent set of structural limits.

Decisions become rule-governed rather than open-ended under boundary conditions. Rule-governed does not imply rigidity in the sense of inflexibility. It implies that decisions are guided by structural rules derived from constraints. These rules define the permissible range of action and provide a framework for evaluation. The system operates within these rules, reducing the need for ad hoc judgment in each instance.

The elimination of bad options is a direct consequence of constraint filtering and boundary definition. Bad options can be defined as those that are misaligned with the system's structure. They may exceed capacity, introduce disproportionate exposure, or violate timing requirements. These options are not necessarily identifiable through detailed evaluation alone, especially in complex environments. Constraints provide a mechanism for excluding them early in the decision process.

By eliminating structurally harmful paths before evaluation, constraints improve the average quality of decisions. The system does not expend resources analyzing options that would lead to instability. Instead, it focuses on options that are within its tolerance range. This early exclusion reduces the likelihood that a decision will introduce significant misalignment, as the most harmful options are removed from consideration.

Removing poor options improves average decision quality because it shifts the distribution of possible outcomes. When bad options are included, the system's decisions are drawn from a wider range that includes both aligned and misaligned paths. When these options are excluded, the range is narrowed to those that are more likely to maintain stability. The system's decisions are therefore more likely to fall within acceptable bounds.

Decision quality improves through exclusion rather than expansion. Expanding the option set increases the number of possible decisions, but it also increases the number of potential errors. Exclusion reduces the number of decisions, but it also reduces the range of possible misalignment. The system's objective is not to maximize the number of options, but to operate within a set of options that are structurally aligned. Constraints achieve this by limiting the decision space.

Elimination reduces exposure to downside risk by removing options that carry disproportionate negative outcomes. These options may appear attractive under certain conditions, particularly if they offer potential gains. However, their inclusion introduces exposure to losses that exceed the system's capacity to absorb them. By excluding these options, constraints reduce the system's sensitivity to extreme outcomes, improving stability.

Constraint filtering, boundary-based evaluation, and elimination of bad options together define the Constraint-Based Decision Mechanism. Each component contributes to the reduction of the decision space to a manageable and structurally aligned subset. Filtering removes infeasible options, boundaries define permissible ranges, and elimination excludes harmful paths. The resulting decision environment is more constrained, but also more coherent.

Constraints reduce the range of possible errors by limiting the set of decisions that can be made. Error can be understood as the set of outcomes that deviate from structural alignment. When the decision space is large, this error space is also large, as there are many ways in which decisions can misalign with the system. When constraints are applied, the decision space contracts, and with it, the range of possible errors.

A smaller decision space increases the probability of alignment because the system operates within a subset of options that are already filtered for structural compatibility. The likelihood that a decision will fall within acceptable bounds is higher when those bounds are enforced prior to evaluation. The system's decisions are therefore more consistently aligned with its requirements, even in the presence of uncertainty and variability.

Error space can be defined as the range of possible misaligned outcomes that can result from the decision process. This space is determined by the size and composition of the option set. A large, unbounded option set creates a wide error space, where decisions can diverge significantly from alignment. A constrained option set compresses this space, limiting the extent to which decisions can deviate from acceptable conditions.

Constraints compress the error space into manageable bounds by restricting the range of possible decisions. This compression does not eliminate error entirely. Misalignment can still occur within the constrained set. However, the magnitude and frequency of error are reduced because the most extreme deviations are no longer possible. The system operates within a narrower band of outcomes, improving stability.

The Constraint-Based Decision Mechanism establishes that constraints function as structural guides rather than as mere limitations. They shape the decision environment by filtering options, defining boundaries, and eliminating misaligned paths. In doing so, they reduce complexity, increase clarity, and improve the probability of alignment. The system's stability is enhanced not by expanding its range of possible actions, but by operating within a structured and constrained space where decisions can be evaluated more effectively.

The Simplification Mechanism

A financial system operates through a network of variables, pathways, and interactions that collectively determine how decisions are formed and how outcomes emerge. The total scope of these elements defines the system's decision surface area. This surface area is not a physical dimension, but a structural one. It represents the number of factors that must be considered, the number of possible paths a decision can take, and the number of interactions that can influence the result. As this surface area expands, the system's complexity increases. As it contracts, the system becomes more coherent.

Decision surface area includes all variables that influence evaluation, all pathways through which decisions can be executed, and all interactions between those variables and pathways. Each additional variable introduces new potential states, each additional pathway introduces new sequences of action, and each interaction introduces new dependencies. The system must account for all of these elements to maintain alignment. As the number of elements grows, the burden on processing capacity increases.

Larger decision surface areas increase both complexity and variability. Complexity arises from the number of elements and their interactions. Variability arises from the number of possible configurations those elements can take. When the system operates across a wide surface area, small changes in inputs can propagate through multiple pathways, producing a wide range of outcomes. The system becomes less predictable because the number of potential trajectories expands.

Reducing variables limits interaction pathways. When the number of variables is reduced, the number of possible interactions decreases at a faster rate. This reduction simplifies the system's internal structure. The system no longer needs to account for interactions that have been removed. The evaluation process becomes more focused, as fewer relationships must be considered. The system's representation of its environment becomes more stable, as there are fewer sources of variation.

A smaller decision surface improves consistency because the system operates within a narrower set of conditions. Consistency depends on the ability to apply similar evaluation processes across different decision cycles. When the surface area is large, each decision may involve a different subset of variables and interactions, leading to variation in evaluation. When the surface area is reduced, the system encounters more similar conditions across cycles, allowing for more uniform application of its decision process.

Reduced surface area stabilizes outcomes by limiting the range of possible deviations. With fewer variables and interactions, the system's behavior becomes more predictable. Outcomes may still vary, but the extent of variation is constrained by the reduced complexity of the system. The system is less sensitive to small changes in inputs because there are fewer pathways through which those changes can propagate.

Standardization introduces consistent structures across decision cycles. It defines patterns that the system applies repeatedly, reducing variation in how decisions are evaluated and executed. Standardization does not eliminate variability in inputs or outcomes, but it stabilizes the process through which decisions are made. The system relies on predefined structures rather than constructing a new evaluation framework for each decision.

Repeated patterns reduce variability in evaluation by providing a consistent method for processing inputs. When the system encounters similar conditions, it applies the same structure, leading to similar evaluations. This reduces the dispersion of decisions that arises from inconsistent processing. The system's behavior becomes more predictable, not because conditions are constant, but because the response to those conditions is standardized.

Standardization lowers processing demand by reducing the need for continuous re-evaluation of decision structures. Without standardization, the system must determine how to evaluate each decision independently, allocating capacity to both the evaluation of inputs and the construction of the evaluation process itself. With standardization, the process is predefined. The system can focus its capacity on interpreting inputs within this structure, rather than on redefining the structure for each decision.

Consistency improves predictability of outcomes because the system's responses become more uniform. When similar inputs are processed through the same structure, the resulting decisions follow similar patterns. This does not eliminate variability in outcomes, as external conditions and stochastic factors still play a role. However, it reduces variability that arises from internal inconsistency in decision-making.

Standardization transforms decisions into repeatable processes. Each decision is not an isolated event, but an instance of a broader pattern. The system applies the same rules, constraints, and evaluation criteria across cycles. This repeatability allows the system to maintain coherence over time, as decisions are aligned with a consistent framework. The system's trajectory becomes more stable because it is shaped by repeated application of the same structural logic.

Unnecessary choices expand the decision space without improving alignment. These choices are options that do not materially contribute to better outcomes, either because they introduce negligible benefit or because they increase complexity without reducing risk. The presence of unnecessary choices increases the number of alternatives that must be considered, adding to the system's processing burden.

Excess choices increase decision complexity by expanding the number of possible paths the system can take. Each additional choice introduces new variables and interactions that must be evaluated. The system must allocate capacity to assess these options, even if they do not materially affect the outcome. This expansion increases the likelihood of overload, as the system's processing capacity is finite.

Removing low-value options reduces noise in the decision environment. Noise consists of inputs and alternatives that do not significantly influence alignment but complicate evaluation. By excluding these options, the system can focus on the variables and pathways that matter most. The signal-to-noise ratio improves, allowing for clearer interpretation of the remaining options.

Fewer choices improve clarity and speed of evaluation. Clarity improves because the system can concentrate on a smaller set of alternatives, each of which can be evaluated more thoroughly. Speed improves because the system does not need to process an extensive set of options before arriving at a decision. These effects are not independent. Reduced complexity allows for both deeper and more efficient evaluation within the same capacity constraints.

Decision quality improves when irrelevant options are excluded because the system's attention is directed toward structurally meaningful alternatives. The presence of irrelevant options dilutes this attention, increasing the likelihood that important variables are overlooked or misinterpreted. By removing these options, the system reduces the risk of misalignment that arises from processing unnecessary complexity.

Reducing decision surface area, standardizing processes, and removing unnecessary choices together define the Simplification Mechanism. Each component contributes to a reduction in system complexity and an increase in decision consistency. The system does not become simpler in the sense of losing necessary structure. It becomes more focused, with its complexity aligned to its processing capacity.

Simplicity stabilizes decision processes by reducing variability in how decisions are generated. When the system operates within a constrained surface area, applies standardized structures, and excludes unnecessary options, it produces decisions that are more consistent across cycles. This consistency does not eliminate error, but it reduces variability in the decision process itself, allowing the system to maintain coherence over time.

Reliability depends on consistency across cycles. A reliable system produces outcomes that are predictable within a defined range, even under varying conditions. This predictability arises from the stability of the decision process, not from the absence of variability in inputs. When the process is consistent, the system's responses to variation are also consistent, allowing for more stable trajectories.

Reliability can be defined as predictable system behavior under variation. The system does not require constant conditions to be reliable. It requires that its decision process produce coherent responses across different states. Simplification supports this by reducing the number of variables and interactions that can introduce inconsistency into the process.

Simplification reduces variability in decision outputs by limiting the sources of variation within the system. With fewer variables, fewer pathways, and standardized processes, the system's decisions are less sensitive to small changes in inputs. The range of possible outputs narrows, and the system's trajectory becomes more stable.

The Simplification Mechanism establishes that reducing complexity is not an objective in itself, but a means of aligning system structure with processing capacity. When complexity exceeds capacity, decision accuracy declines. When complexity is reduced to a manageable level, the system can process information coherently, maintain consistency across cycles, and produce more reliable outcomes.

As the system evolves, the balance between necessary complexity and manageable simplicity determines its stability. Complexity cannot be eliminated entirely, as it reflects the reality of the system's environment.

However, it can be structured in a way that aligns with the system's capacity. Simplification is the process through which this alignment is achieved, reducing unnecessary variation and stabilizing the decision process.

In this context, simplicity is not the absence of structure. It is the presence of structure that is coherent, repeatable, and aligned with the system's limits. Decisions made within such a structure are not only easier to evaluate, but more consistent in their outcomes. The system's behavior becomes more predictable, and its ability to maintain stability under varying conditions is strengthened.

The Pre-Commitment Mechanism

A decision is not defined solely by what is chosen, but by when the choice is formed relative to the conditions under which it is executed. Timing introduces a structural dimension into decision systems, separating the formation of a decision from its application. In many cases, these two phases occur simultaneously. A condition emerges, the system evaluates it under existing constraints, and a decision is produced in response. This alignment of formation and execution places the decision within the same environment that contains pressure, variability, and incomplete information. Pre-commitment alters this alignment by shifting decision formation to an earlier state, where these conditions are less restrictive.

Pre-commitment can be defined as the process of establishing decisions prior to the moment in which they must be executed. The decision is formed in advance, based on anticipated conditions, structural rules, or predefined criteria, and is then applied later when those conditions arise. This separation changes the environment in which the decision is made. Formation occurs under one set of conditions, while execution occurs under another. The difference between these environments determines how the decision interacts with the system.

Early decisions occur under conditions of lower pressure and higher clarity. When the system is not operating near its constraints, it has greater capacity to process information, evaluate alternatives, and consider longer time horizons. Inputs are more stable, and the system is less affected by urgency or scarcity. The decision process can therefore incorporate a broader set of variables and a more coherent evaluation framework. The resulting decision reflects a state in which constraints are less binding and variability is less disruptive.

Design separates decision-making from execution by creating a structural distinction between the two phases. In a reactive system, decision-making is embedded within execution. The system evaluates and acts simultaneously, with both processes influenced by the same constraints. In a pre-committed system, decision-making is relocated to an earlier stage. Execution becomes the application of a prior decision rather than the creation of a new one. This separation reduces the influence of execution conditions on the formation of the decision.

Decisions made in stable conditions are structurally stronger because they are formed with greater informational completeness and lower constraint pressure. Stability does not imply the absence of uncertainty, but it implies that the system is not operating under compressed conditions. The system can evaluate decisions without the distortions introduced by urgency, scarcity, or volatility. As a result, the decision is more aligned with the system's structure rather than with the immediate pressures of the environment.

The timing of decision formation affects outcome quality because it determines which conditions influence the evaluation process. A decision formed under stable conditions is influenced by broader considerations and longer time horizons. A decision formed under pressure is influenced by immediate constraints and limited capacity. The difference in timing leads to differences in how variables are weighted, how options are considered, and how alignment is achieved. The same decision executed under the same conditions may produce different outcomes depending on when it was formed.

Real-time variability refers to the fluctuation of inputs and conditions during the moment of execution. These fluctuations include changes in resource availability, timing mismatches, external disturbances, and internal constraints. When decisions are made in real time, they must incorporate these unstable inputs into the evaluation process. The system must interpret conditions that are changing while the decision is being formed, reducing clarity and increasing the likelihood of misalignment.

Decisions made in the moment are affected by pressure, scarcity, and volatility because these conditions are most pronounced at the point of execution. Pressure compresses time, limiting evaluation depth. Scarcity reduces available options and capacity to absorb error. Volatility alters inputs, making projections less reliable. When decision-making occurs within this environment, it inherits these distortions. The decision reflects the constraints of the moment rather than the system's broader structure.

Pre-commitment removes dependence on unstable conditions by relocating decision formation to a period where these conditions are less influential. The system defines its response to future states in advance, based on structural considerations rather than immediate inputs. When the execution condition arrives, the decision is already determined. The system does not need to evaluate the situation fully in real time. It applies the pre-committed rule or structure.

Execution becomes less sensitive to fluctuating inputs because the decision does not rely on interpreting those inputs at the moment they occur. Variability still affects outcomes, but it does not alter the decision itself. The system's response is predetermined, reducing the impact of input fluctuations on decision formation. This does not eliminate variability in results, but it stabilizes the process through which decisions are applied.

Variability is reduced when decisions are predetermined because the system's response becomes consistent across similar conditions. Without pre-commitment, each instance of a condition may produce a different decision, depending on how inputs are interpreted in real time. With pre-commitment, the system applies the same response each time the condition arises, reducing variation in decision outputs. This consistency contributes to stability across decision cycles.

Commitment structures are the mechanisms that enforce prior decisions at the point of execution. They translate pre-commitment into action by constraining the system's ability to deviate from the established decision. These structures may take the form of rules, automated processes, contractual obligations, or predefined sequences of action. Their function is to ensure that the decision formed in advance is applied consistently when the relevant conditions occur.

Commitment structures constrain future decision flexibility by limiting the system's ability to revise or override the pre-committed decision at the moment of execution. This constraint is not incidental. It is the mechanism through which pre-commitment maintains its effectiveness. Without constraint, the system could revert to real-time decision-making under pressure, reintroducing the conditions that pre-commitment is designed to avoid.

Constraints applied in advance reduce reactive behavior by removing the need for full evaluation under execution conditions. The system does not need to interpret every variable in real time. It follows the structure defined by the commitment. This reduces the influence of transient conditions on decision-making, allowing the system to operate with greater consistency across different states.

Commitments stabilize system behavior across time by creating continuity between decision cycles. Each execution of the pre-committed decision reinforces the system's trajectory, reducing variability in how similar conditions are handled. The system's behavior becomes more predictable, as it is guided by predefined structures rather than by ad hoc responses to each instance of variability.

Commitment strength determines adherence to prior decisions. Strength refers to the degree to which the commitment structure prevents deviation at the point of execution. A strong commitment leaves little room for adjustment, ensuring that the pre-committed decision is applied consistently. A weaker commitment allows for greater flexibility, but also increases the possibility that the system will revert to reactive decision-making under pressure. The balance between commitment and flexibility defines how the system integrates pre-commitment into its operation.

Advance decision design, removal of real-time variability, and commitment structures together define the Pre-Commitment Mechanism. Each component shifts decision-making away from reactive environments and toward controlled environments. Advance design relocates decision formation to a state of lower constraint. Removal of real-time variability reduces the influence of unstable inputs. Commitment structures enforce consistency at the point of execution. The interaction of these elements changes how decisions function within the system.

Decisions made earlier occur under better conditions because they are formed when the system is not constrained by immediate pressure or variability. The system has greater capacity to evaluate, more stable inputs to consider, and more time to integrate information. These conditions allow for decisions that are more aligned with the system's structure and less influenced by transient factors.

Execution quality depends on when decisions are made because the conditions at the time of formation determine how the decision is structured. A decision formed under stable conditions carries that structure into execution, even when conditions become unstable. A decision formed under unstable conditions reflects the constraints and distortions present at that moment. The timing of formation therefore has a direct effect on the quality of execution.

Timing is a structural variable in decision systems. It defines the environment in which decisions are formed and the conditions under which they are applied. By altering the timing of decision formation, the system alters the factors that influence evaluation. This change is not marginal. It affects how decisions are constructed, how they interact with variability, and how they contribute to the system's trajectory.

Earlier decisions reduce pressure-induced errors by removing the need to evaluate under compressed conditions. When decisions are made in advance, the system does not need to process information under urgency or scarcity at the point of execution. The potential for misalignment introduced by these conditions is reduced. The decision reflects the system's structure rather than the distortions of the moment.

The Pre-Commitment Mechanism establishes that the timing of decision formation is as important as the content of the decision itself. By shifting decisions to earlier stages, the system changes the conditions under which they are made, reducing the influence of pressure, variability, and constraint. Execution becomes an application of prior structure rather than a reaction to current conditions. As decisions accumulate, this shift in timing contributes to greater consistency, reduced error, and increased stability across the system's trajectory.

The Margin for Error Mechanism

A financial system does not operate in a state of perfect alignment. Decisions are made under constraint, outcomes diverge from expectations, and variability introduces deviations that cannot be fully anticipated or controlled. Error is therefore not an exception within the system. It is a continuous output of its operation. The system's stability is not determined by the absence of error, but by how that error interacts with its structure. The presence or absence of margin for error defines whether deviations remain contained or propagate into failure.

Buffers represent the structural capacity reserved for absorbing deviation and error. They are not incidental surpluses that exist outside the system's core operation. They are integral components that define how the system responds when outcomes differ from expectations. A buffer exists as a layer between normal operation and constraint thresholds, intercepting deviations before they reach points of structural failure. This separation is not static. It is defined by the size and configuration of the buffer relative to the system's exposure.

The presence of buffers creates distance between the system's operating state and its failure thresholds. Failure thresholds represent conditions beyond which the system cannot maintain continuity. When a system operates without buffers, this distance is minimal or nonexistent. Any deviation moves the system directly toward or into failure. When buffers are present, deviations are absorbed within the intermediate space. The system continues to operate within its tolerance range, even as conditions fluctuate.

Buffer size determines the system's tolerance range. Tolerance range refers to the magnitude of deviation the system can absorb without crossing into instability. A larger buffer extends this range, allowing the system to withstand greater misalignment. A smaller buffer constrains it, reducing the system's capacity to absorb variation. The system's response to error is therefore not uniform. It is scaled by the depth of its buffers.

Systems without buffers transmit error directly into instability because there is no intermediate capacity to contain deviation. When an outcome diverges from expectation, the effect is immediate and unmediated. The system must adjust in real time to prevent failure, often under conditions of pressure and constraint. This direct transmission increases the likelihood that errors will compound, as each deviation interacts with a system already operating near its limits.

Buffer design defines system resilience. Resilience is not an abstract property. It is the measurable capacity of the system to absorb deviation without structural failure. The configuration of buffers—how much capacity is reserved, where it is positioned, and how it interacts with other components—determines how the system responds to error. A system with well-defined buffers can absorb repeated deviations while maintaining stability. A system without such design is sensitive to even small misalignments.

Overcapacity extends the concept of buffers by defining the total capacity available beyond immediate operational requirements. It represents the portion of the system's resources that are not committed to current obligations. This excess capacity is not idle. It provides the system with flexibility, allowing it to absorb variability, adjust to changing conditions, and respond to error without immediate consequence.

Excess capacity allows for variability and misalignment by creating space within which deviations can occur. When the system is not operating at full capacity, it can tolerate fluctuations in inputs and outputs. Variability does not immediately disrupt its operation because the system has unused resources that can be mobilized to compensate for discrepancies. This capacity acts as a buffer against both expected and unexpected changes.

Systems operating at full capacity have zero tolerance for error. In such systems, all resources are allocated to meeting current obligations. There is no reserve to absorb deviation. Any misalignment, regardless of magnitude, requires immediate adjustment. The system becomes highly sensitive to variability, as it lacks the capacity to accommodate even minor fluctuations. Stability in this state is contingent on perfect alignment, which cannot be sustained under real-world conditions.

Overcapacity provides flexibility under uncertainty by allowing the system to operate without immediate constraint. Uncertainty introduces variability in both inputs and outcomes. When capacity exceeds immediate requirements, the system can respond to this variability without compressing decision timelines or reducing option sets. It retains the ability to evaluate, adjust, and sequence decisions over time, rather than being forced into reactive behavior.

Margin for error is a function of unused capacity. It is not determined by the system's total resources, but by the portion of those resources that remain available to absorb deviation. A system with significant resources but no unused capacity has no margin for error. Conversely, a system with moderate resources but substantial unused capacity may have a meaningful margin for error. The distinction lies in how capacity is allocated relative to obligations.

Error absorption is the process through which the system contains misalignment without allowing it to propagate into structural failure. When an error occurs, it introduces a discrepancy between expected and actual conditions. Absorption occurs when this discrepancy is contained within the system's buffers, preventing it from affecting core operations or pushing the system beyond its thresholds.

Absorbed errors do not propagate through the system because their effects are contained within the buffer layer. The system can adjust internally, reallocating resources or modifying subsequent actions, without altering its overall structure. The error is effectively neutralized within the system's tolerance range. This containment prevents the error from influencing other components or from triggering additional deviations.

Absorption prevents cascading effects by isolating deviations from the broader system. Cascading occurs when an error in one component propagates to others, creating a chain reaction of misalignment. When buffers are present, they interrupt this propagation. The error is absorbed before it can interact with other variables or pathways. The system remains stable, even though the initial deviation occurred.

Systems differ in how they respond to the same error based on their capacity for absorption. A deviation that is absorbed in one system may lead to instability in another, depending on the size and configuration of their buffers. The error itself is not the determining factor. The system's ability to contain it defines the outcome. This distinction highlights that stability is not a function of avoiding error, but of managing its effects.

Absorption stabilizes trajectory under repeated deviations. Financial systems do not experience isolated errors. Deviations occur continuously, as decisions are made under uncertainty and conditions fluctuate. A system with sufficient absorption capacity can withstand this sequence of deviations without significant change in its trajectory. Each error is contained, allowing the system to maintain coherence over time. A system without this capacity accumulates the effects of deviations, leading to gradual or abrupt shifts in its trajectory.

Buffers, overcapacity, and absorption together define the Margin for Error Mechanism. Each component contributes to the system's ability to tolerate misalignment without failure. Buffers provide the space within which deviations can be contained. Overcapacity ensures that resources are available to support this containment. Absorption defines the process through which errors are neutralized within the system's structure. The interaction of these elements determines how the system responds to variability.

Resilience depends on tolerance, not on the elimination of error. Tolerance refers to the range of deviation the system can absorb without crossing its failure threshold. A resilient system is one that maintains operation within this range, even as errors occur. It does not require perfect alignment. It requires sufficient capacity to contain misalignment.

Tolerance defines how much error a system can absorb because it establishes the boundary between normal operation and failure. Within this boundary, the system can adjust, absorb, and continue functioning. Beyond it, the system cannot recover without structural change. The position of this boundary is determined by the system's buffers and overcapacity. The wider the tolerance range, the more resilient the system.

Failure threshold represents the point beyond which the system cannot sustain its operation. It is not a gradual transition. It is a boundary condition where the system's structure is no longer sufficient to absorb deviation. When this threshold is crossed, the system must undergo significant adjustment or ceases to function within its prior configuration. The threshold is defined by the limits of capacity, exposure, and constraint.

Margin for error determines proximity to this threshold. A system with significant margin operates at a distance from its failure point, allowing it to absorb deviations without approaching instability. A system with minimal margin operates close to the threshold, where even small deviations can push it beyond its limits. The system's stability is therefore not defined by its current state alone, but by its position relative to its thresholds.

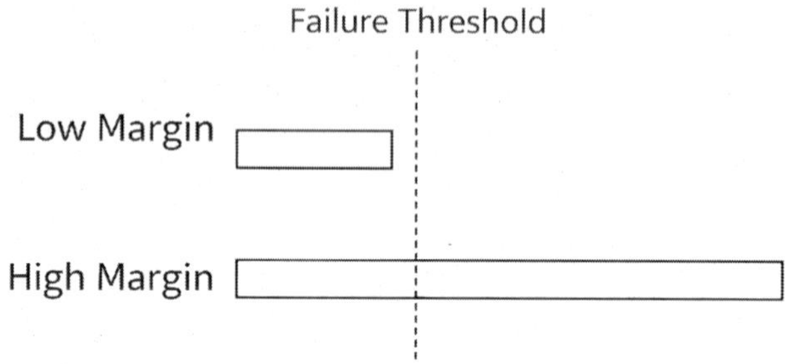

[Figure 3: Margin vs Failure Threshold]

The relationship between margin and failure threshold can be represented as a continuum of deviation along a horizontal axis. As deviation increases, the system moves closer to a vertical boundary representing the failure threshold. The region before this boundary defines the absorption zone, where errors are contained within the system's buffers. Within this zone, the system operates within tolerance, maintaining stability despite misalignment. Beyond the boundary, the system enters a failure state, where it can no longer absorb additional deviation.

The trajectory of the system can be visualized as a path moving through this space. Each decision and outcome introduces variation, shifting the system's position along the axis. When margin is present, the trajectory remains within the absorption zone, even as deviations occur. When margin is limited, the trajectory approaches the threshold more rapidly, increasing the likelihood of crossing into failure.

The Margin for Error Mechanism establishes that stability is a function of how much deviation a system can absorb, not how effectively it avoids deviation. Errors are inevitable within decision systems. The structural question is whether those errors remain within the system's tolerance range or push it beyond its capacity to recover. Buffers, overcapacity, and absorption define this range, shaping how the system interacts with variability over time.

As decisions accumulate, the system's position relative to its thresholds changes. Each deviation, whether absorbed or transmitted, influences this position. A system with sufficient margin maintains a stable trajectory, as errors are contained within its buffers. A system without margin experiences increasing sensitivity to deviation, as each error moves it closer to its threshold. The difference between these systems is not the presence or absence of error, but the capacity to absorb it without structural failure.

The Decision Framework Mechanism

A financial system does not generate decisions in isolation. Each decision emerges from a process that interprets inputs, applies evaluation criteria, and produces an output that alters the system's trajectory. The structure of this process determines how consistently decisions are formed across time. When the process is unstructured, each decision is evaluated independently, often under varying conditions and with shifting criteria. When the process is structured, decisions are produced through a repeatable framework that organizes inputs and defines how they are interpreted. The presence or absence of this structure introduces a fundamental difference in how decisions function within the system.

Structured evaluation can be defined as the use of predefined processes for decision-making. These processes establish a consistent method for interpreting inputs, weighting variables, and determining outcomes. The framework does not eliminate the need for evaluation. It defines how evaluation occurs. Each decision is processed through the same structure, regardless of the specific conditions under which it is made. This consistency transforms decision-making from an ad hoc activity into a system function.

Structure organizes inputs by defining which variables are relevant and how they are incorporated into the evaluation process. In an unstructured system, inputs may be considered in varying combinations, with different variables emphasized in different instances. This variability introduces inconsistency in how decisions are formed. In a structured system, inputs are processed according to a defined pattern. The same categories of information are considered, and their relationships are evaluated within a consistent framework. This organization reduces ambiguity in how inputs influence decisions.

Structured evaluation reduces ambiguity by limiting the degrees of freedom in interpretation. Ambiguity arises when multiple interpretations of the same inputs are possible, each leading to different decisions. By defining how inputs are processed, the framework constrains these interpretations. The system does not need to determine how to evaluate each variable in every instance. It applies the predefined structure, reducing uncertainty in the evaluation process itself.

Consistent frameworks improve clarity across decisions because they create a stable reference for interpretation. When the same process is applied repeatedly, the system's understanding of how inputs translate into decisions becomes more coherent. Clarity is not derived from the absence of uncertainty in inputs, but from the consistency of the process used to interpret them. The system can distinguish between variability in inputs and variability in evaluation, allowing it to respond more predictably to changing conditions.

Structure stabilizes how decisions are formed by reducing variation in the process itself. Decisions may still differ in their outcomes due to differences in inputs, but the method by which those outcomes are produced remains constant. This stability allows the system to maintain coherence across decision cycles, even as conditions fluctuate. The system's trajectory is shaped by a consistent logic, rather than by a sequence of unrelated or inconsistent decisions.

Randomness within decision systems can be defined as variation in outputs that arises from inconsistent processes rather than from differences in inputs. When decisions are made without a structured framework, the process itself becomes a source of variability. Two identical sets of inputs may produce different decisions because they are evaluated differently in each instance. This variability is internal to the system, reflecting the absence of consistent structure.

Ad hoc decisions introduce variability independent of inputs because they rely on context-specific evaluation. Each decision is influenced by the conditions present at the moment, including pressure, time constraints, and the subset of information that is immediately available. These factors alter how inputs are interpreted, leading to variation in decision outputs that does not correspond to variation in the underlying conditions. The system's behavior becomes less predictable, as it is influenced by both external variability and internal inconsistency.

Consistency reduces internally generated variation by stabilizing the evaluation process. When decisions are produced through a structured framework, the process itself does not introduce additional variability. Differences in outcomes can be attributed more directly to differences in inputs, rather than to fluctuations in how those inputs are interpreted. This separation allows the system to respond more accurately to changes in its environment.

Outcomes reflect inputs more accurately under consistent processes because the mapping between inputs and decisions is stable. In an unstructured system, this mapping is variable, making it difficult to determine whether differences in outcomes are due to changes in inputs or changes in evaluation. In a structured system, the mapping is fixed, allowing the system to isolate the effect of input variability on outcomes. This improves the system's ability to interpret its own behavior.

Frameworks reduce noise created by inconsistent evaluation by eliminating variation in the decision process that is unrelated to inputs. Noise in this context refers to fluctuations in decision outputs that do not correspond to meaningful differences in conditions. By applying a consistent structure, the system filters out this noise, allowing the underlying signal—variation in inputs—to be more clearly reflected in decisions. The system's behavior becomes more transparent and more stable.

Decision sequencing refers to the order in which decisions are made and applied within the system. Decisions do not exist as isolated events. Each decision influences subsequent decisions, either by altering the system's state or by defining the context in which future decisions are evaluated. The sequence in which decisions occur therefore affects how they interact and how their effects accumulate over time.

Structured sequencing organizes decisions into a coherent order, aligning them with the system's temporal and structural requirements. Without structure, decisions may be made in response to immediate conditions, without regard for their interaction with prior or subsequent decisions. This can lead to misalignment, as decisions may conflict or interfere with each other. Structured sequencing defines the order in which decisions should occur, ensuring that they build upon each other in a consistent manner.

The order of decisions affects how they interact over time. A decision that is appropriate in one sequence may produce different outcomes if applied in another. For example, decisions that alter capacity, exposure, or timing can change the conditions under which subsequent decisions are made. Structured sequencing accounts for these interactions, aligning decisions in a way that maintains coherence across time. The system's trajectory is shaped not only by individual decisions, but by their order and interaction.

Frameworks align decisions across time horizons by integrating sequencing into the decision process. Short-term and long-term considerations are incorporated into a consistent structure, ensuring that decisions made at different points in time are compatible with each other. This alignment reduces the risk of decisions that are locally consistent but globally misaligned, where short-term actions conflict with long-term stability.

Proper sequencing reduces compounding misalignment by ensuring that each decision contributes to a coherent trajectory. When decisions are made without regard to sequence, misalignments can accumulate, as each decision introduces discrepancies that are not corrected in subsequent steps. Structured sequencing organizes decisions in a way that minimizes these discrepancies, reducing the likelihood that small misalignments will compound into larger structural issues.

Structured evaluation, consistency in process, and coherent sequencing together define the Decision Framework Mechanism. Each component contributes to the stabilization of decision-making within the system. Structured evaluation defines how inputs are processed, consistency reduces internally generated variability, and sequencing aligns decisions across time. The interaction of these elements creates a framework through which decisions are produced in a repeatable and coherent manner.

Frameworks stabilize decision processes across cycles by ensuring that each decision is generated through the same structure. This stability does not eliminate variability in inputs or outcomes, but it ensures that the process itself does not introduce additional variation. The system's behavior becomes more predictable because it is governed by a consistent set of rules and sequences, rather than by ad hoc responses to each instance of variability.

Reduced variability in the decision process improves predictability of outcomes because it isolates the sources of variation. When the process is stable, differences in outcomes can be attributed to differences in inputs or external conditions. The system can therefore anticipate how changes in these factors will influence its trajectory. Predictability is not the ability to forecast exact outcomes, but the ability to understand how the system responds to variation.

Frameworks can be defined as repeatable decision systems. They encapsulate the structure, criteria, and sequence through which decisions are made, allowing the system to apply the same logic across multiple instances. This repeatability is essential for maintaining coherence over time, as it ensures that decisions are aligned with a consistent framework rather than with transient conditions.

Stability arises from process consistency, not from control over outcomes. Outcomes are influenced by external variability, randomness, and incomplete information. These factors cannot be fully controlled by the system. What can be controlled is the process through which decisions are made. By stabilizing this process, the system reduces the internal sources of variability that can amplify external uncertainty.

As decisions accumulate, the presence of a framework determines how they interact and how their effects propagate through the system. A structured framework aligns decisions across time, reduces noise in evaluation, and stabilizes the system's trajectory. Without such a framework, decisions are more likely to diverge, introducing variability that is independent of the system's environment.

The Decision Framework Mechanism establishes that reliability in decision systems is not achieved by eliminating uncertainty or variability in inputs. It is achieved by stabilizing the process through which decisions are generated and applied. Frameworks provide this stability by organizing evaluation, enforcing consistency, and aligning sequencing. The system's ability to maintain coherence under variation depends on the presence of such structures, as they define how decisions function within the broader system.

The Default Path Mechanism

A financial system does not require continuous intervention to produce outcomes. Once configured, it operates through embedded pathways that execute without active decision input. These pathways are not temporary. They persist as structural features, carrying forward prior configurations into future states. The Default Path Mechanism describes how these pathways function as the system's baseline mode of operation, determining what occurs when no overriding decision is introduced.

Automation represents the structural continuity of these pathways. Within a system, automation can be defined as the execution of processes that have been predefined, requiring no additional evaluation at the point of action. These processes are established through prior decisions, encoded into the system's structure, and repeated across time. Once in place, they operate independently of real-time analysis, translating prior configuration into ongoing execution.

Automated processes create predefined flows that govern how resources, obligations, and actions move through the system. These flows are not static in content, but they are stable in form. They repeat according to established rules, producing recurring patterns of behavior. The system does not re-evaluate these flows each time they occur. Instead, it relies on the embedded structure to execute them consistently.

Continuity is maintained without evaluation because the system's design substitutes prior decision-making for present analysis. The decision has already been made at the point of configuration. Each subsequent execution is not a new decision, but the continuation of that initial choice. The system operates as if the decision is being made repeatedly, but in reality, it is being carried forward without reconsideration.

Automation therefore functions as embedded decision execution. It transforms discrete decisions into continuous processes, extending their influence across time. The system's behavior becomes less dependent on active input and more dependent on its existing configuration. This shift reduces the need for constant evaluation, but it also means that the system's trajectory is determined by decisions that may no longer be actively considered.

Passive decisions emerge when the system continues to operate without intervention. A passive decision is not an explicit choice. It is the outcome of not altering the system's existing pathways. When no active decision is made to change the system's direction, the system continues along its current trajectory. This continuation is itself a form of decision execution, even though it lacks deliberate input at the moment of action.

In the absence of intervention, the system does not pause. It proceeds according to its existing structure. Each automated process, each predefined flow, and each embedded rule continues to operate. The system's state evolves as these processes unfold, producing outcomes that are consistent with its configuration. Non-intervention does not suspend decision-making. It allows the system's prior decisions to continue executing.

Continuation of existing trajectories is therefore the default condition of the system. Each moment builds upon the previous one, with no requirement for active reassessment. The system's direction is maintained through the persistence of its pathways. Changes occur only when these pathways are altered. Until such alteration takes place, the system follows the path defined by its current structure.

Non-decision functions as decision execution because the system's processes remain active regardless of whether new input is provided. The absence of intervention does not eliminate decision-making. It shifts the source of decisions from the present to the past. The system executes decisions that were made earlier, without requiring confirmation or reconsideration in the current moment.

Passive continuation reflects the persistence of prior structure. The system's configuration carries forward, influencing each subsequent state. This persistence creates stability in the sense of continuity, but it also creates inertia. The system does not naturally diverge from its established path. It remains aligned with the decisions that defined its current configuration, unless an active change is introduced.

Default behaviors arise from these persistent pathways. A default behavior is the action or outcome that occurs when no alternative is selected. It represents the baseline response of the system to a given set of conditions. Defaults are not created at the moment of execution. They are formed through prior decisions, embedded into the system, and activated whenever the relevant conditions are present.

Defaults are established through the accumulation of prior configurations. Each decision that sets a rule, defines a process, or creates a pathway contributes to the system's default behavior. Over time, these contributions form a network of defaults that govern how the system operates. The system does not need to generate new decisions for each situation. It applies its existing defaults.

Reinforcement occurs as defaults are executed repeatedly. Each execution strengthens the pathway, making it more entrenched within the system's structure. This reinforcement is not necessarily intentional. It is a consequence of repeated use. The more frequently a default is executed, the more central it becomes to the system's operation.

Path dependency emerges from this reinforcement. The system's current state is shaped by the sequence of defaults that have been executed over time. Each default builds upon the previous ones, creating a trajectory that reflects the system's history. Changing this trajectory requires altering the underlying defaults, which are embedded within the system's structure.

Defaults function as the baseline operating mode. They define how the system behaves under normal conditions, without requiring active decision input. This baseline is not neutral. It reflects the cumulative effect of prior decisions and configurations. The system's behavior is therefore shaped more by its defaults than by isolated, active decisions.

The system moves along the path of least resistance because it follows the pathways that require the least effort, energy, or structural change to execute. These pathways are typically the defaults, as they are already embedded within the system. No additional configuration is required to activate them. They represent the easiest available route for the system to follow.

Minimization of effort and constraint drives the persistence of these paths. Introducing a new pathway requires overcoming structural resistance, reallocating resources, and altering existing configurations. In contrast, continuing along the default path requires no such adjustment. The system therefore remains aligned with its existing pathways unless a sufficient force is applied to change them.

Default paths persist even when misaligned because the system does not inherently evaluate alignment at each step. It executes its embedded processes regardless of whether they remain optimal under current conditions. Misalignment may develop gradually, as conditions change and the default path no longer corresponds to the system's requirements. However, the system continues along this path because it is the lowest-friction option.

Structural inertia reinforces this persistence. Inertia refers to the system's tendency to maintain its current state. Once a pathway is established, it becomes part of the system's structure. Changing it requires overcoming the inertia created by its integration with other components. This resistance makes default paths stable, even when they are no longer aligned with the system's environment.

Altering established paths is difficult because it requires disrupting the existing structure. The system must not only create a new pathway but also dismantle or override the old one. This process involves reconfiguring dependencies, adjusting flows, and reallocating resources. The complexity of this reconfiguration contributes to the persistence of default paths.

Repeated execution of default decisions produces cumulative effects over time. Each instance of execution may appear minor in isolation, but the aggregation of these instances defines the system's trajectory. The system does not rely on large, singular decisions to determine its direction. It evolves through the continuous application of its defaults.

Small, consistent outputs accumulate, creating significant changes in the system's state. These outputs are not necessarily the result of active intent. They emerge from the repeated execution of default processes. The system's trajectory is therefore shaped by patterns of behavior that operate continuously, rather than by isolated events.

Default-driven trajectory formation reflects the dominance of these patterns. The system follows a path defined by its defaults, with each execution reinforcing the direction established by prior configurations. This trajectory may align with the system's objectives, or it may diverge from them, depending on the alignment of the defaults themselves.

Drift occurs when the system continues along a default path that is not actively evaluated. This drift is not abrupt. It develops gradually, as the cumulative effect of default execution moves the system away from its desired state. Because the process is continuous and incremental, the drift may not be immediately visible.

Outcomes emerge without active intent because the system does not require explicit decisions to produce results. The execution of defaults generates outcomes as a byproduct of ongoing processes. The system's state changes over time, reflecting the influence of these processes, even in the absence of deliberate action.

Defaults that were formed under prior conditions persist into new environments. The system does not automatically update its pathways when conditions change. It continues to operate according to its existing configuration, unless an active decision is made to alter it. This persistence creates a structural lag between the system's behavior and its current environment.

This lag leads to misalignment when the default path no longer corresponds to the system's requirements. The system may continue to follow a pathway that was appropriate under previous conditions but is no longer suitable. Because the pathway is embedded, the system does not adjust automatically. Misalignment accumulates as the environment diverges from the conditions under which the defaults were formed.

Unexamined continuation of outdated structures reinforces this misalignment. The system does not inherently assess whether its defaults remain appropriate. It executes them as designed. Without active evaluation, the system may carry forward structures that introduce inefficiencies, increase exposure, or reduce stability.

Latent risk is embedded within default behavior when misalignment is present. This risk is not always immediately visible. It may remain dormant until certain conditions trigger its effects. The system's exposure to this risk is determined by the nature of the defaults and the extent to which they diverge from current requirements.

Resistance to changing defaults arises from their integration within the system. Defaults are not isolated components. They are connected to other processes, dependencies, and flows. Altering a default requires addressing these connections, which increases the complexity of change.

Switching costs and friction contribute to this resistance. Changing a default pathway involves reallocating resources, modifying processes, and potentially disrupting ongoing operations. These costs create a barrier to change, reinforcing the persistence of the existing path.

Disruption is required to alter default behavior because the system must break from its established trajectory. This disruption is not limited to a single decision. It involves reconfiguring the structure that supports the default, ensuring that the new pathway can be sustained over time.

Dependency chains reinforce defaults by linking multiple processes to the same pathway. A change in one part of the system may require changes in others, as dependencies are interconnected. This interdependence increases the effort required to modify defaults, further entrenching them within the system.

System reconfiguration is necessary to establish new defaults. This reconfiguration involves redefining processes, adjusting flows, and creating new pathways that can operate without continuous intervention. The system must be restructured so that the new defaults become the path of least resistance.

Default paths interact with other mechanisms within the system, amplifying or moderating their effects. Under conditions of scarcity, defaults may reinforce constrained behavior, as the system lacks the capacity to deviate from its established pathways. Under conditions of margin, the system may have greater flexibility to override defaults, allowing for alternative trajectories.

Pre-commitment interacts with defaults by intentionally setting the pathways that the system will follow in the absence of intervention. Frameworks formalize these pathways, embedding them within structured processes. The interaction between these mechanisms determines how defaults are established, maintained, and altered.

Under pressure, default paths may become more dominant. The system's capacity for active decision-making is reduced, increasing reliance on existing pathways. This reliance amplifies the influence of defaults, as the system executes them without reevaluation.

The stability or instability of the system depends on the structure of its defaults. If defaults are aligned with the system's requirements, they contribute to stability by producing consistent, appropriate outcomes. If they are misaligned, they introduce drift and increase exposure to risk.

Outcomes are largely determined by what occurs without intervention. Active decisions may alter the system's trajectory, but they are not the primary driver of its behavior. The baseline behavior defined by default pathways operates continuously, shaping the system's direction over time.

The system's trajectory is defined by its baseline behavior. Each execution of a default contributes to this trajectory, reinforcing the direction established by prior configurations. Active decisions act as overrides, temporarily altering the path, but the system returns to its defaults once these interventions cease.

The structural importance of baseline pathways lies in their persistence. They operate continuously, independent of active input, making them the dominant force in determining long-term outcomes. The system's behavior is therefore a function of its defaults, rather than of isolated decisions.

The Default Path Mechanism establishes that systems do not require continuous decision-making to produce outcomes. They operate through embedded pathways that execute automatically, defining what occurs in the absence of intervention. Stability depends on how these pathways are structured, as they determine the system's trajectory over time. Misaligned defaults produce drift without visible decision points, shaping outcomes through continuous execution rather than through discrete actions.

The Feedback Delay Mechanism

A financial system relies on feedback to interpret the relationship between decisions and outcomes. Feedback provides information about how a prior action has translated into a result, allowing the system to adjust its trajectory over time. This process is foundational to learning within the system. However, the timing of feedback is not synchronized with the timing of decisions. Outcomes do not become visible at the moment of execution. They emerge later, often after additional decisions have already been made. This temporal gap defines the Feedback Delay Mechanism.

Feedback can be defined as the information returned to the system regarding the outcome of a prior decision relative to its intended or expected effect. It functions as a signal that informs whether the system's trajectory is aligned or misaligned with its structure. In an idealized environment, feedback would arrive immediately, allowing the system to observe the direct consequences of its actions. In practice, this immediacy does not exist. There is always a lag between the point at which a decision is executed and the point at which its outcome becomes observable.

This lag is structural. Financial systems operate through processes that unfold over time. Transactions settle, obligations mature, and interactions between variables propagate through multiple stages before producing visible results. The system cannot observe the full effect of a decision until these processes have completed. As a result, feedback is inherently delayed. The system must continue operating in the absence of complete information about the consequences of its prior actions.

The distinction between immediate and delayed feedback environments is critical. In environments with immediate feedback, the system can directly link decisions to outcomes, reinforcing or correcting behavior in near real time. In delayed environments, this linkage is weakened. The system receives information about outcomes only after a period has passed, during which additional decisions have been made. The sequence of decisions and outcomes becomes interwoven, making it difficult to isolate the effect of any single action.

The temporal separation between cause and effect arises from this delay. Decisions occur at a specific point in time, while their outcomes emerge later. The system operates continuously, producing new decisions before the outcomes of previous ones are fully visible. This creates overlapping layers of cause and effect, where multiple decisions contribute to the same observable result.

Because decisions and outcomes exist in different time frames, the direct connection between them is weakened. The system cannot easily trace a specific outcome back to a specific decision. Instead, outcomes reflect the combined effect of multiple prior actions, each interacting with evolving conditions. The causal chain becomes distributed across time, reducing the clarity of the relationship between input and result.

Tracing outcomes back to their originating decisions becomes increasingly difficult as the number of intervening steps grows. Each step introduces additional variables and interactions that influence the final result. The system must reconstruct the causal pathway after the fact, attempting to determine which decisions contributed to the observed outcome. This reconstruction is inherently uncertain, as it relies on incomplete information and retrospective interpretation.

Multi-step interactions further complicate this process. A decision may initiate a sequence of effects that unfold through intermediate stages, each influenced by other variables. The final outcome is not the result of a single decision, but of a chain of interactions that extend over time. The system must account for these interactions when interpreting feedback, but the delay in feedback obscures their structure.

Misinterpretation arises when the system incorrectly attributes outcomes to causes. Because feedback arrives after a delay, the system may associate an outcome with the wrong decision or set of conditions. Intervening variables that were not present at the time of the decision may influence the outcome, leading to incorrect conclusions about causality.

The presence of confounding factors increases the likelihood of misinterpretation. External variability, changes in conditions, and interactions between variables all contribute to the outcome. When feedback is delayed, these factors may be mistaken for the primary cause of the result. The system's interpretation is therefore based on a mixture of relevant and irrelevant influences.

Reconstruction of cause after the outcome appears introduces additional distortion. The system observes the result and attempts to infer the decisions that produced it. This process is inherently retrospective, relying on the system's ability to recall and analyze prior states. However, the passage of time and the accumulation of additional decisions reduce the accuracy of this reconstruction. The system may emphasize certain variables while overlooking others, leading to incomplete or incorrect interpretations.

Retrospective bias emerges as the system attempts to impose coherence on delayed feedback. The system seeks to explain outcomes in a way that appears consistent with its understanding of prior decisions. This can lead to overconfidence in the inferred causal relationship, even when the underlying connection is uncertain. The system's interpretation becomes shaped by the outcome itself, rather than by an accurate reconstruction of the causal process.

Feedback signals are not purely informational. They contain both signal and noise. The signal represents the meaningful information about the relationship between decision and outcome, while noise represents the influence of unrelated or random factors. In delayed feedback environments, the distinction between signal and noise becomes less clear.

External variability introduces distortion into feedback signals. Changes in conditions that occur after the decision has been made can influence the outcome, adding noise to the feedback. The system must differentiate between the effect of the original decision and the effect of subsequent variability. This differentiation is difficult when feedback is delayed, as the system lacks a clear temporal boundary between cause and effect.

Isolating meaningful information becomes more complex as noise increases. The system must filter out irrelevant influences to identify the signal that reflects the decision's impact. However, the delay in feedback reduces the system's ability to perform this filtering accurately. The signal may be obscured by noise, leading to incomplete or misleading interpretations.

The system tends to overweight recent or visible signals because they are more accessible at the time of evaluation. Delayed or indirect signals, which may be more relevant to the original decision, are underweighted because they are less apparent. This imbalance further distorts the system's interpretation of feedback, as it prioritizes immediacy over accuracy.

Reinforcement is the process through which the system adjusts future decisions based on observed outcomes. It relies on feedback to determine whether prior decisions were aligned or misaligned. When feedback is delayed, reinforcement is also delayed. The system does not receive timely information about the consequences of its actions, slowing the adjustment process.

The delay between decision and reinforcement signal means that the system continues to operate without correction. Multiple decisions may be made before the system receives feedback about earlier actions. Each of these decisions is influenced by incomplete information, increasing the likelihood of misalignment.

Slow correction of misalignment results from this delay. The system cannot adjust its trajectory until feedback becomes available. By the time reinforcement occurs, the system may have already moved further along a path that reflects earlier misalignment. The correction must then address not only the initial deviation but also the additional effects that have accumulated.

Reinforcement arriving after multiple decisions have occurred weakens the learning loop. The system's ability to associate outcomes with specific decisions is reduced, as the feedback reflects the combined effect of several actions. The adjustment process becomes less precise, as the system cannot isolate the contribution of individual decisions.

Incorrect reinforcement patterns emerge when feedback is misinterpreted. Positive outcomes may reinforce decisions that were not actually responsible for the result, while negative outcomes may discourage decisions that were structurally sound. This misalignment in reinforcement arises from the delay and distortion in feedback signals.

When a positive outcome is observed, the system may attribute it to the most recent or most visible decision, rather than to the actual cause. This leads to reinforcement of a pathway that may not be aligned with the system's structure. Conversely, when a negative outcome occurs, the system may attribute it to a decision that was not responsible, leading to the abandonment of a path that was structurally appropriate.

Reinforcement based on incomplete information creates feedback loops that diverge from the system's requirements. The system adjusts its behavior in response to perceived patterns that do not accurately reflect the underlying causal relationships. Over time, these incorrect adjustments accumulate, leading to drift.

Drift occurs as the system repeatedly reinforces incorrect patterns. Each reinforcement shifts the system's trajectory slightly, and the accumulation of these shifts produces a significant divergence from the intended path.

Because the reinforcement is based on delayed and distorted feedback, the system may not recognize the misalignment until it becomes pronounced.

The compounding effects of feedback delay arise from the accumulation of uncorrected errors. Each decision made before feedback arrives carries the potential for misalignment. Without timely correction, these misalignments accumulate, influencing subsequent decisions and outcomes.

As multiple decisions are made in the absence of feedback, the system's trajectory diverges from its intended path. The divergence is not immediately visible, as feedback has not yet revealed the misalignment. When feedback eventually arrives, it reflects the combined effect of these decisions, making it difficult to isolate the source of the deviation.

Reduced ability to course-correct results from this accumulation. The system must address not only the initial error but also the additional misalignments that have developed. The correction process becomes more complex, as it must account for the compounded effects of multiple decisions.

Feedback delay interacts with other mechanisms within the system, amplifying their effects. Time horizon distortion increases the difficulty of aligning decisions with long-term outcomes, as delayed feedback obscures the connection between present actions and future results. Default paths reinforce existing trajectories, making it more likely that delayed feedback will perpetuate misalignment. Complexity increases the number of variables and interactions, adding noise to feedback signals. Volatility introduces additional variability, further distorting the relationship between decision and outcome.

Under conditions of uncertainty, these interactions amplify misinterpretation. The system must operate with incomplete information, delayed signals, and fluctuating inputs. The combined effect reduces clarity, making it more difficult to interpret feedback accurately.

Feedback delay functions as a structural constraint on learning. The system cannot adjust its behavior until feedback becomes available, and the quality of that adjustment depends on the clarity of the feedback signal. Because feedback is delayed and noisy, the system's learning process is inherently limited.

The system cannot learn faster than feedback allows. Even if the system increases its evaluation capacity, it cannot accelerate the arrival of feedback. The timing of feedback is determined by the underlying processes that produce outcomes, which cannot be compressed without altering the system's structure.

Learning is therefore bounded by feedback timing. The system's ability to adapt depends on how quickly and accurately it can interpret the consequences of its decisions. Delayed feedback slows this process, while noisy feedback reduces its accuracy. The combination limits the system's capacity to align its trajectory with its structure.

The Feedback Delay Mechanism establishes that feedback is necessary but imperfect. It provides information about outcomes, but this information is delayed and distorted. The system must interpret feedback despite these limitations, attempting to link cause and effect across time. Because this linkage is weakened, learning is slower and less precise.

The system operates continuously, making decisions in the absence of complete feedback. Each decision contributes to the system's trajectory, even as the consequences of prior decisions remain partially unknown. Stability depends on the system's ability to function under these conditions, relying on structure rather than immediate outcome interpretation.

Feedback cannot be relied upon at the moment decisions are made. The system must operate in advance of its own understanding, adjusting only after outcomes have already shaped its trajectory.

The Drift Mechanism

Drift describes the gradual movement of a system away from its intended alignment. It is not a discrete shift, but a continuous process in which small deviations accumulate over time. Each deviation may appear negligible when observed in isolation, but their combined effect alters the system's trajectory. This movement occurs without a single identifiable point of failure. Instead, the system transitions through states of increasing misalignment, often remaining functional even as its structural coherence deteriorates.

Drift must be distinguished from sudden failure. Failure is an event, marked by the system crossing a threshold beyond which it cannot maintain operation. Drift is the process that precedes such an event. It unfolds incrementally, without clear boundaries, making it difficult to identify at early stages. The system does not move from stability to failure in a single step. It moves through a spectrum of alignment, where each incremental change contributes to a gradual divergence from its original configuration.

Alignment within a system is not binary. It does not exist solely as a state of being either correct or incorrect. It exists along a continuum, where the system may be partially aligned or partially misaligned. Small deviations shift the system along this continuum, often without triggering immediate consequences. Because these shifts are minor, they remain below the system's visibility threshold. The system continues to operate, and the deviation becomes part of its evolving structure.

Misalignment often begins before it is observable. Early-stage drift does not produce outcomes that clearly indicate structural divergence. The system's outputs may still fall within acceptable ranges, masking the underlying change. This creates a condition where drift progresses without detection, embedding itself within the system's operation. By the time misalignment becomes visible, it has already accumulated through multiple iterations.

Deviation is the fundamental unit of drift. It represents the difference between the system's expected state and its actual state following a decision or external change. Deviations arise from imperfect decisions, variability in conditions, and incomplete information. Each deviation introduces a small discrepancy into the system. When these discrepancies are not corrected, they persist and interact with subsequent decisions.

Accumulation occurs as deviations are layered over time. Each new decision is made within a system that has already been altered by prior deviations. The system's state is therefore not static. It evolves continuously, incorporating the effects of each deviation into its structure. This layering process shifts the system's trajectory, even if individual deviations are small.

The accumulation of deviation is closely linked to delayed feedback. Because feedback about outcomes is not immediate, the system continues to operate without full knowledge of its current alignment. Decisions are made before the consequences of prior actions are fully understood. This delay allows deviations to persist and multiply, as the system lacks the information required to correct them in real time.

Default pathways further reinforce accumulation. In the absence of active intervention, the system continues along its existing trajectory. Deviations embedded within this trajectory are carried forward, becoming part of the system's baseline behavior. The system does not pause to reassess its alignment. It proceeds according to its structure, allowing deviations to compound through repeated execution.

Compounding misalignment emerges from this process. It is not the result of a single large error, but of many small deviations that interact over time. Each deviation shifts the system slightly, and the accumulation of these shifts produces a significant divergence. The trajectory of the system changes gradually, reflecting the compounded effect of its prior states.

Control within a system can be defined as its ability to maintain alignment within a defined tolerance range. This ability depends on the system's capacity to detect deviation and adjust its trajectory accordingly. As drift accumulates, this capacity is reduced. The system's actual state diverges from its intended state, increasing the dispersion between expected and realized outcomes.

As misalignment grows, the reliability of decision inputs declines. The system's evaluation processes rely on assumptions about its current state. When the system is misaligned, these assumptions become less accurate. Decisions are made based on incomplete or distorted representations of reality, further increasing the likelihood of additional deviation.

Variability and complexity amplify this effect. As inputs become noisier and interactions between variables increase, the system's ability to interpret its state diminishes. Drift introduces additional uncertainty into the system, making it more difficult to distinguish between normal variation and structural misalignment. The system's responses become less precise, contributing to further divergence.

Recognition of drift typically occurs after a delay. The system does not immediately identify misalignment as it develops. Instead, it detects the consequences of drift once they reach a level that affects observable outcomes. This delay reduces the system's ability to correct its trajectory efficiently. By the time misalignment is recognized, it has already progressed beyond its initial stages.

Control degradation is therefore a lagging indicator. It reflects the accumulated effect of prior deviations rather than a real-time measure of alignment. The system appears stable until the effects of drift become pronounced. When instability emerges, it is often the result of a long period of unobserved divergence.

Drift is not an exceptional condition within a financial system. It is an inherent feature of operation. All systems experience drift because they operate under conditions of imperfect information, variable environments, and delayed feedback. Decisions are never perfectly aligned with outcomes, and conditions are never static. These factors ensure that deviation is continuously introduced into the system.

Static stability is not achievable under these conditions. A system cannot remain perfectly aligned over time without adjustment. External conditions change, internal configurations evolve, and interactions between variables produce new states. Drift arises from these dynamics, reflecting the system's movement through an environment that is constantly in flux.

Time horizon distortion and feedback delay contribute to this inevitability. Decisions are evaluated based on incomplete information about future outcomes, and feedback arrives after a delay. The system cannot fully anticipate or immediately correct deviations. As a result, drift becomes the default direction of movement in the absence of intervention.

Drift should therefore be understood as the baseline condition of unmanaged systems. It is not a sign of failure, but a consequence of operating within real-world constraints. The system moves away from alignment unless active measures are taken to maintain it. Stability is not maintained automatically. It requires continuous adjustment.

The interaction between drift and other system mechanisms determines its rate and impact. Default pathways reinforce existing trajectories, including those that are misaligned. Feedback delay slows the system's ability to recognize and correct deviation. Scarcity constrains the system's capacity to respond effectively, often leading to decisions that exacerbate misalignment. Complexity obscures the sources of drift, making it more difficult to identify the underlying causes. Volatility increases the variability of outcomes, amplifying deviation. Pre-commitment can either stabilize the system by setting aligned pathways or lock in misalignment if the initial structure is flawed.

These interactions ensure that drift is not an isolated process. It is embedded within the broader system architecture, influenced by multiple mechanisms that either accelerate or moderate its progression. The system's trajectory is shaped by the combined effect of these interactions, rather than by drift alone.

The progression of drift can be visualized as a gradual movement away from alignment over time. Along a temporal axis, the system's alignment level decreases incrementally, reflecting the accumulation of small deviations. Occasional corrections may occur, temporarily improving alignment, but the overall trend continues downward if deviations are not fully addressed. The contrast between this trajectory and an idealized path of stable alignment highlights the effect of uncorrected drift.

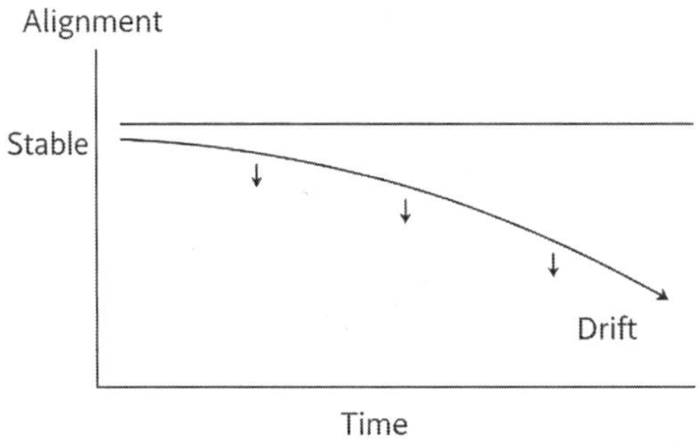

[Figure 4: Decision Drift Over Time]

Drift is difficult to detect in its early stages because it operates below visibility thresholds. Small deviations are often indistinguishable from normal variability. The system interprets them as routine fluctuations rather than as indicators of structural change. This interpretation delays recognition, allowing drift to progress unnoticed.

Feedback delay further obscures detection. The system does not receive immediate information about the consequences of its decisions, making it difficult to link observed outcomes to specific causes. As a result, the system may normalize gradual decline, incorporating it into its expectations of normal operation.

Recognition typically occurs after meaningful divergence has already taken place. The system becomes aware of misalignment when its effects are large enough to influence observable outcomes. At this point, the system is no longer close to its original alignment. The correction required is therefore more significant.

The cost of correction increases as drift accumulates. Early-stage corrections involve small adjustments that can be made within the system's existing structure. Late-stage corrections require more substantial changes, as the system's configuration has been altered by accumulated deviations. These changes may involve reconfiguring processes, reallocating resources, or modifying constraints.

Accumulated deviation increases the effort required for correction. The system must address not only the initial misalignment but also the additional discrepancies that have developed over time. This increases the complexity of the adjustment process, as multiple layers of deviation must be resolved simultaneously.

System disruption becomes more likely as correction costs increase. Larger adjustments may interfere with ongoing operations, introducing additional variability and potential for error. The system must balance the need for correction with the risk of destabilizing its current state.

Margin for error plays a critical role in this process. Systems with greater buffer capacity can absorb deviations and implement corrections more gradually. Systems with limited margin must make more abrupt adjustments, increasing the risk associated with correction. The availability of capacity therefore influences both the feasibility and the effectiveness of realignment.

The increase in correction difficulty is nonlinear. Small increases in drift may require disproportionately larger adjustments to restore alignment. This nonlinearity reflects the compounding nature of deviation and the structural changes it introduces. The system's ability to correct its trajectory diminishes as drift progresses.

Recalibration is the process through which the system restores alignment in response to drift. It involves adjusting the system's structure, updating its assumptions, and modifying its pathways to reflect current conditions. Recalibration is not a response to failure. It is a response to the ongoing process of drift.

Stability is maintained through recalibration rather than through static optimization. The system cannot achieve a permanent state of alignment. It must continuously adjust to account for new information, changing conditions, and accumulated deviations. Recalibration is therefore an ongoing process, integrated into the system's operation.

This process depends on the system's ability to interpret feedback, evaluate its constraints, and redesign its structure where necessary. It requires the system to recognize drift and respond before misalignment becomes critical. The effectiveness of recalibration determines the system's ability to maintain control over time.

Drift establishes that systems do not remain aligned automatically. They move away from alignment through the accumulation of small deviations, influenced by delayed feedback, default pathways, and variable conditions. Control degrades gradually, reflecting the system's increasing distance from its intended state. Stability is not a fixed property, but a dynamic condition that must be maintained through continuous recalibration.

The Liquidity Buffer Mechanism

A financial system does not operate solely on the presence of resources, but on the accessibility and timing of those resources relative to its obligations. Liquidity defines this accessibility. It represents the portion of capacity that can be deployed immediately to sustain the system's operation without requiring structural change. While often interpreted as a stock of available capital, liquidity functions more precisely as time. It determines how long the system can continue operating before it is forced to alter its structure in response to constraint.

Runway emerges from this relationship between available capacity and ongoing demand. It represents the duration for which the system can sustain its current state given its rate of consumption. Liquidity provides the resource base, while the system's ongoing requirements determine how quickly that base is consumed. The result is not simply a quantity, but a time horizon. This horizon can be measured conceptually in units of operation—days, weeks, or months during which the system can continue without requiring immediate adjustment.

The distinction between stock and flow clarifies this function. Liquidity is a stock, representing accumulated accessible capacity at a point in time. Income or inflow represents a flow, describing the rate at which resources enter the system. A system may have high inflow but limited liquidity, or substantial liquidity but variable inflow. It is liquidity that determines the system's immediate ability to operate without disruption.

Flow contributes to long-term capacity, but does not define the system's present time horizon.

Liquidity converts uncertainty into time by providing a buffer against variability in inflows and outflows. When uncertainty is present, outcomes cannot be predicted with precision. Liquidity allows the system to continue operating while this uncertainty resolves, extending the period during which decisions can be made. Without this buffer, uncertainty compresses the system's time horizon, forcing immediate responses.

The length of runway directly influences decision quality because it determines the time available for evaluation. Decisions are not formed in isolation from their temporal context. When the system has extended runway, it can allocate more time to processing information, comparing alternatives, and sequencing actions. This extended evaluation window improves the conditions under which decisions are formed.

Short runway environments produce a different set of conditions. The system must act within narrow time constraints, limiting its ability to integrate information or explore multiple pathways. Decisions are made with reduced evaluation depth, as the system prioritizes immediate continuity over structural alignment. The difference between these environments is not inherent to the system's design, but to its available time.

Extended runway reduces the influence of short-term bias by allowing decisions to incorporate longer time horizons. When the system is not constrained by immediate deadlines, it can evaluate outcomes across a broader temporal range. This reduces the weighting of immediate results relative to longer-term effects, improving alignment between decisions and system stability.

Scarcity pressure operates in the opposite direction, compressing the time available for decision-making. Liquidity counteracts this compression by extending the system's operational horizon. The presence of liquidity allows decisions to be made without the immediate pressure of constraint, improving the conditions under which they are evaluated.

More time allows for more complete information integration. Data that would otherwise be unavailable at the moment of decision can be incorporated as it becomes visible. The system can observe trends, interpret signals, and adjust its evaluation based on evolving conditions. This process improves the accuracy of decision inputs.

The ability to compare alternatives depends on the availability of time. In compressed environments, the system may not have the capacity to evaluate multiple pathways. With extended runway, alternatives can be considered in parallel, allowing the system to select among a broader set of feasible options. This comparison improves the likelihood of alignment between decision and system requirements.

Sequencing decisions properly also depends on time. Certain decisions are interdependent, requiring a specific order to maintain coherence. Extended runway allows the system to align decisions in a sequence that reflects their structural relationships. Without sufficient time, sequencing is disrupted, and decisions may be executed in an order that introduces misalignment.

Urgency emerges as a function of proximity to constraint. When the system approaches a threshold beyond which it cannot sustain operation, time becomes compressed. This compression creates a condition in which decisions must be made immediately, regardless of the completeness of available information or the quality of evaluation.

Low liquidity brings the system closer to this threshold, increasing urgency. The system must respond quickly to maintain continuity, reducing its ability to evaluate decisions thoroughly. This environment prioritizes immediacy over alignment, as the primary objective becomes avoiding disruption.

High liquidity increases the distance between the system's current state and its constraint thresholds. This distance extends the time available before action is required. Decisions can therefore be made independently of immediate necessity, allowing the system to operate without constant time pressure.

Urgency reduces evaluation depth by limiting the time available to process information. It also reduces the system's ability to explore options, as the need for immediate action constrains the range of feasible alternatives. Decision accuracy declines as a result, not because of inherent deficiencies in the system, but because of the conditions under which decisions are made.

Liquidity removes urgency by extending the time before constraint forces action. This does not eliminate the need for decisions, but it changes the conditions under which they are made. Decisions can be formed under less compressed conditions, improving their structural alignment.

Optionality refers to the range of viable paths available to the system at any given point. This range is not static. It depends on the system's capacity, constraints, and time horizon. Liquidity expands optionality by allowing the system to maintain multiple potential trajectories simultaneously.

Delayed decisions become possible when liquidity is present. The system is not required to commit immediately to a single path. It can defer action until additional information becomes available or until conditions are more favorable. This deferral preserves flexibility, allowing the system to adjust its trajectory as new information emerges.

Staged execution is another function of expanded optionality. Decisions can be implemented in phases, rather than as single, irreversible actions. Each stage provides additional information about the system's response, allowing subsequent stages to be adjusted accordingly. This approach reduces the risk associated with uncertainty.

Tolerance for temporary misalignment increases with liquidity. The system can absorb deviations without immediate correction, maintaining stability while evaluating the appropriate response. This tolerance does not eliminate misalignment, but it prevents it from forcing immediate structural change.

Constrained systems lose options because they lack the capacity to maintain multiple pathways. When liquidity is limited, the system must commit to a course of action quickly, reducing its ability to adapt. Optionality is therefore directly linked to available time, as options require the capacity to delay commitment.

Liquidity and capacity are closely related in this context. The presence of excess capacity allows the system to sustain multiple potential states, each representing a different trajectory. This capacity is expressed as time, which provides the window within which options can exist.

The contrast between liquidity and scarcity highlights their structural roles. Scarcity compresses time, forcing decisions to be made quickly and under constraint. It narrows the range of feasible options, limiting the system's ability to adapt. Liquidity expands time, allowing decisions to be made under less constrained conditions and increasing the range of available options.

Decision quality is therefore environment-dependent. The same system will produce different outcomes depending on whether it operates under conditions of liquidity or scarcity. Under scarcity, decisions are reactive and constrained. Under liquidity, decisions are more deliberate and aligned with the system's structure.

Liquidity transforms the decision environment by altering the conditions under which decisions are made. It does not change the system's underlying mechanisms, but it changes how those mechanisms operate. The presence of time allows the system to function with greater coherence, reducing the influence of constraint on decision-making.

Drift, as a process of accumulated deviation, is influenced by the system's capacity to detect and correct misalignment. Liquidity provides the time required for this detection and correction to occur at earlier stages.

When the system has sufficient runway, it can identify small deviations before they compound into larger structural issues.

Early correction reduces the magnitude of adjustment required. Small deviations can be addressed incrementally, maintaining alignment without significant disruption. Liquidity enables this process by providing the time necessary to evaluate and implement corrections.

Low liquidity environments force corrections to occur at later stages, when deviations have already accumulated. The system must then implement larger adjustments to restore alignment, increasing the risk of disruption and error. The timing of correction is therefore a function of available liquidity.

Margin for error is directly related to this capacity for correction. Liquidity contributes to this margin by extending the system's ability to absorb deviation without immediate consequence. This extension allows the system to maintain stability while adjusting its trajectory.

Decision timing is influenced by the relationship between liquidity and constraint. In the absence of liquidity, decisions are aligned with deadlines. The system must act when required, regardless of whether conditions are optimal. With sufficient liquidity, decisions can be aligned with conditions rather than with immediate necessity.

Timing flexibility allows the system to separate decision formation from execution. Decisions can be made when information is more complete and conditions are more stable, rather than when constraints force action. This separation improves the structural quality of decisions.

The ability to choose when to act influences the outcome of decisions. Timing affects the availability of information, the range of options, and the level of pressure within the system. Liquidity provides the capacity to align timing with these factors, improving the conditions under which decisions are made.

Liquidity does not eliminate uncertainty, error, or variability. These elements are inherent to financial systems and cannot be removed through the presence of capacity alone. Liquidity modifies the conditions under which these factors are managed, but it does not remove them from the system.

Excess liquidity without structural alignment can introduce inefficiencies. The system may delay necessary actions, allowing misalignment to persist. Drift may continue if liquidity is not used to correct deviations. The presence of time does not guarantee alignment. It provides the opportunity for alignment to be maintained.

Liquidity must therefore operate within the system's structure. It enhances the system's ability to respond to variability, but it does not define the system's direction. The effectiveness of liquidity depends on how it is integrated with other mechanisms, including decision frameworks, constraints, and feedback processes.

Stability within a financial system requires the ability to evaluate decisions, absorb variability, and adjust to changing conditions. Each of these functions depends on the availability of time. Liquidity provides this time by extending the system's runway, allowing it to operate without immediate constraint.

As runway extends, urgency decreases, improving the conditions under which decisions are made. Improved decision conditions lead to greater alignment between decisions and system requirements. This alignment stabilizes the system's trajectory, reducing the accumulation of deviation.

Optionality expands under liquidity, providing the system with multiple pathways through which to respond to uncertainty. Drift can be identified and corrected earlier, preventing small deviations from compounding into larger structural issues. The system maintains coherence through its ability to adapt within an extended time horizon.

Liquidity functions as a stabilizer of decision quality, a reducer of error frequency, and a buffer against forced action. It does not eliminate the challenges inherent in financial systems, but it changes how those challenges are managed. By converting capacity into time, liquidity alters the environment in which decisions are formed and executed.

The Liquidity Buffer Mechanism establishes that time is the primary condition under which decision quality improves. Liquidity extends this time, reducing urgency, expanding optionality, and allowing decisions to be made under less constrained conditions. Systems with sufficient liquidity do not eliminate uncertainty, but they operate within it more effectively. Stability is not achieved by avoiding variability, but by having the time required to respond to it with precision.

The Income Stability Mechanism

A financial system operates through a sequence of inflows and outflows distributed across time. These inflows represent the primary inputs that sustain the system's capacity to meet obligations and maintain continuity. Income, in this context, is not a single event but a recurring pattern of resource entry. The structure of this pattern—specifically its consistency in timing and magnitude—determines the stability of the system's input layer. The Income Stability Mechanism defines how this consistency reduces variability, providing a predictable baseline against which decisions are formed and executed.

Income stability is not defined by the size of inflows, but by their predictability. Two dimensions determine this predictability. Magnitude stability refers to the consistency of the amount received across periods, while timing stability refers to the regularity of intervals between inflows. A system may exhibit stability in one dimension but not the other. For example, inflows may be consistent in size but irregular in timing, or consistent in timing but variable in magnitude. True stability emerges when both dimensions align, producing a pattern that can be anticipated with minimal uncertainty.

This pattern establishes a baseline inflow structure. The baseline functions as a reference point, allowing the system to interpret its current state relative to expected conditions. When inflows follow a predictable pattern, the system can assume continuity in its resource availability. This assumption simplifies the evaluation of decisions, as it reduces the number of unknown variables that must be considered.

The presence of a stable baseline changes how the system operates. Decisions are no longer made against an uncertain backdrop of fluctuating inputs. Instead, they are made relative to a consistent expectation of resource availability. This expectation anchors the system, providing a foundation upon which other processes can be built.

Variability in inflows introduces uncertainty into the system. When the timing or magnitude of inflows fluctuates, the system cannot rely on a stable reference point. Each period must be evaluated independently, as prior patterns may not hold. This variability disrupts the sequencing of decisions, as the system must continuously adjust to changing conditions.

Reduced variability at the input level simplifies system interpretation. When inflows are stable, changes in the system's state can be attributed more directly to other factors. The system does not need to account for fluctuations in its primary inputs when evaluating outcomes. This clarity improves the system's ability to interpret signals, as it can isolate the effects of decisions and external variables more effectively.

The distinction between environmental variability and input variability is critical. Environmental variability refers to changes in external conditions that affect the system, such as market fluctuations or unexpected events. Input variability refers to changes in the system's own inflows. While environmental variability cannot be fully controlled, input variability can be structured. Reducing variability at the input level does not eliminate uncertainty, but it narrows the range within which the system must operate.

As input variability decreases, the dispersion of possible system states is reduced. The system's range of outcomes becomes more concentrated around its baseline, making it easier to predict and manage. This reduction in dispersion enhances the system's ability to maintain alignment, as it operates within a more constrained set of conditions.

Decision stress emerges from the interaction of uncertainty, timing mismatch, and resource unpredictability. When inflows are unstable, the system must make decisions under conditions where future resource availability is unclear. This uncertainty increases the pressure on decision-making, as the system must account for a wider range of potential outcomes.

Timing mismatch occurs when the availability of resources does not align with the timing of obligations. Unstable income increases the likelihood of this mismatch, as inflows may arrive too early or too late relative to the system's requirements. This misalignment forces the system to adjust in real time, increasing the frequency of decisions that must be made under pressure.

Resource unpredictability amplifies this effect. When the system cannot anticipate the magnitude of inflows, it must prepare for multiple scenarios simultaneously. This preparation requires additional evaluation, increasing the cognitive and structural load on the system. Decisions must be made with incomplete information, reducing their accuracy and alignment.

Stable income reduces these pressures by providing a predictable pattern of resource availability. The system can anticipate when inflows will occur and how much they will provide. This predictability reduces the need for reactive decisions, as the system does not need to continuously adjust to unexpected changes in its input layer.

The compression of evaluation windows is also reduced under stable conditions. When inflows are predictable, decisions can be made with sufficient time for analysis and comparison. The system is not forced to act immediately to accommodate variability. This extended evaluation window improves the quality of decisions, as they are formed under less constrained conditions.

Planning within a financial system involves sequencing decisions across time to achieve a coherent trajectory. This process depends on the ability to project future states based on current information. Predictable inputs are essential for this projection, as they provide a stable foundation upon which assumptions can be built.

Stable income anchors these projections by providing a consistent reference for resource availability. The system can model future states with greater confidence, as it does not need to account for significant variability in its primary inputs. This anchoring reduces the dispersion of possible scenarios, allowing the system to focus on a narrower range of outcomes.

In deterministic planning environments, inputs are assumed to be stable, and outcomes can be projected with relatively high precision. In probabilistic environments, inputs are variable, and outcomes must be considered as distributions rather than fixed points. Income stability shifts the system closer to the deterministic end of this spectrum, improving the reliability of planning.

When inputs are unreliable, planning accuracy degrades. The system must incorporate a wider range of assumptions, increasing the complexity of its projections. This complexity introduces additional sources of error, as each assumption carries uncertainty. Stable inputs reduce this complexity, simplifying the planning process and improving alignment between decisions and outcomes.

Timing alignment within the system depends on the synchronization of inflows and outflows. Obligations occur at specific intervals, requiring resources to be available at corresponding times. When income timing is stable, this synchronization can be achieved more easily. The system can align its inflows with its obligations, maintaining coherence in its operation.

Irregular income disrupts this alignment. When inflows do not occur at predictable intervals, the system must adjust its sequencing to accommodate mismatches. These adjustments introduce additional decisions, increasing the complexity of the system's operation. The lack of synchronization creates gaps that must be managed through other mechanisms, such as liquidity.

Stable timing reduces these mismatches by establishing a consistent rhythm within the system. Decisions can be sequenced in a way that reflects this rhythm, improving coherence across time. The system's operations become more predictable, as the timing of resource availability aligns with the timing of obligations.

Income stability and liquidity operate as complementary mechanisms within the system. Liquidity represents a stock of accessible capacity, providing a buffer that extends the system's time horizon. Income stability represents a flow, providing consistent inputs that sustain the system's operation over time.

Liquidity addresses short-term gaps by allowing the system to continue operating when inflows are insufficient or delayed. Income stability reduces the frequency of these gaps by providing predictable inflows. When income is stable, the system relies less on liquidity to maintain continuity. Conversely, when income is unstable, liquidity becomes more critical, as it must compensate for variability in inflows.

The interaction between these mechanisms defines the system's stability. Liquidity provides time, allowing the system to absorb variability and make decisions under less constrained conditions. Income stability provides consistency, reducing the variability that must be absorbed. Together, they create a system that can operate with both flexibility and predictability.

Optionality within the system depends on the persistence of available pathways over time. Stable income supports this persistence by providing a reliable foundation for planning. When inflows are predictable, the system can maintain longer sequencing chains, as it can anticipate the resources required to sustain them.

This predictability enables the system to commit to multi-stage decision frameworks. Decisions can be structured across multiple periods, with each stage building upon the previous one. The system does not need to continuously reassess its ability to sustain these commitments, as the input layer remains stable.

Reduced need for defensive positioning is another consequence of stable inflows. When income is unpredictable, the system must maintain flexibility to respond to potential shortfalls. This flexibility often comes at the cost of reduced commitment to long-term pathways. Stable income reduces this need, allowing the system to operate with greater coherence.

Predictable inflows therefore allow options to persist over time. The system can maintain multiple potential trajectories, selecting among them as conditions evolve. This persistence enhances the system's ability to adapt, as it retains the capacity to shift between pathways without immediate constraint.

Income stability does not eliminate risk, structural misalignment, or decision error. These elements are inherent to the system and arise from factors beyond input consistency. A system with stable income can still experience misalignment if its decisions are not structured appropriately or if its obligations exceed its capacity.

Stable but insufficient income introduces constraint despite predictability. The system may operate within a consistent pattern, but if the magnitude of inflows is inadequate, it will still face pressure. Stability in this case does not equate to sufficiency. The system's requirements must be evaluated relative to its input structure.

Over-reliance on stability can mask inefficiencies within the system. When inflows are predictable, the system may not immediately detect structural misalignment, as its operations continue without disruption. This continuity can delay necessary adaptation, allowing inefficiencies to persist.

Income stability must therefore be evaluated within the broader system context. It improves the conditions under which decisions are made, but it does not define the system's alignment. The interaction between inputs, obligations, and decision structures determines overall stability.

A stable financial system requires predictable inputs, manageable variability, and coherent planning. Income stability contributes to each of these requirements by providing a consistent inflow pattern. This consistency reduces the stress placed on decision-making, allowing the system to operate with greater clarity.

Reduced variability improves interpretability, enabling the system to distinguish between meaningful signals and noise. This clarity enhances decision quality, as the system can evaluate inputs and outcomes with greater precision. Planning becomes more reliable, as projections are anchored in stable assumptions.

The reduction in decision stress further stabilizes the system's operation. Decisions are made under less constrained conditions, reducing the likelihood of reactive responses. The system maintains alignment more effectively, as it operates within a predictable environment.

Income stability functions as a stabilizer of system inputs and a reducer of volatility exposure. By narrowing the range of variability at the input level, it creates conditions under which the system can operate coherently across time. The interaction between stable inflows and other mechanisms determines the system's ability to maintain alignment.

The Income Stability Mechanism establishes that predictability at the input level reduces the variability that destabilizes decision-making. When inflows are consistent in timing and magnitude, the system can operate against a stable baseline, improving planning reliability and reducing the pressure under which decisions are made. Stability in income does not eliminate uncertainty, but it narrows the range within which the system must operate, allowing for greater coherence across time.

The Expense Control Mechanism

The Expense Control Mechanism describes how the regulation of outflows determines the rate at which a system consumes its available capacity and approaches constraint. Expenses function as continuous outflows that interact directly with the system's resource base. Where inflows introduce capacity into the system, outflows remove it. This interaction defines the system's operational balance across time. Income represents the incoming flow of resources, but it does not determine system stability in isolation. Expenses define how quickly those resources are depleted. The relationship between inflow and outflow establishes whether the system expands, maintains, or contracts its available capacity.

Expense control can be defined as the regulation of outflow magnitude, timing, and variability relative to system capacity. This regulation does not imply reduction in all cases. It refers to the alignment of outflows with the system's ability to sustain them. When outflows are structured in a way that exceeds or closely matches capacity, the system operates under pressure. When outflows are regulated below capacity, the system retains flexibility. Expenses therefore determine how quickly the system approaches constraint thresholds. They define the burn structure of the system, translating capacity into time depletion. As outflows increase, the duration for which the system can operate without adjustment decreases.

The composition of expenses introduces an additional structural dimension. Fixed expenses are recurring, time-bound obligations that exhibit low flexibility once established. They persist across periods and require fulfillment regardless of changes in system conditions. Variable expenses, in contrast, represent adjustable outflows that can respond to shifts in capacity or external conditions. These two categories do not differ only in form, but in how they influence the system's responsiveness to pressure.

Fixed expenses create structural rigidity by embedding obligations into the system that cannot be easily modified in the short term. Because they recur at defined intervals, they impose a predictable but inflexible demand on capacity. This rigidity constrains the system's ability to adjust its outflows in response to variability. When capacity is reduced or uncertainty increases, fixed expenses continue to require fulfillment, reducing the system's margin for adaptation.

Variable expenses introduce adaptability by allowing outflows to adjust with changing conditions. They provide a mechanism through which the system can reduce its consumption rate when capacity is constrained. This flexibility allows the system to maintain alignment without requiring immediate structural change. The presence of variable expenses therefore increases the system's ability to respond to stress before reaching critical thresholds.

The balance between fixed and variable expenses determines the system's responsiveness. A system with a high proportion of fixed expenses exhibits limited flexibility under stress, as its obligations are largely predetermined. A system with a greater proportion of variable expenses can adjust its outflows more dynamically, preserving capacity when conditions deteriorate. Expense composition therefore defines how the system behaves when exposed to pressure. Systems dominated by fixed obligations are more sensitive to disruption, while those with variable structures can adapt without immediate failure.

Expense pressure emerges from the rate at which outflows consume available capacity. It represents the speed at which the system moves toward constraint thresholds. Higher expense levels accelerate this movement by increasing the rate of capacity depletion. Lower expense levels slow it, extending the time horizon over which the system can operate without adjustment. This relationship exists independently of inflow magnitude. Two systems with identical income can experience different levels of pressure based on their expense structures.

As expenses rise relative to capacity, the system's proximity to constraint thresholds increases. This proximity compresses the time available for decision-making, as the system must act before capacity is exhausted. Decision timelines become shorter, reducing the opportunity for evaluation and sequencing. Expense pressure therefore translates directly into urgency, not through changes in inflow, but through the rate of outflow.

Expenses convert capacity into time depletion by determining how quickly resources are consumed. The same level of capacity can sustain different durations of operation depending on the expense structure. A system with lower expenses extends its operational time horizon, while a system with higher expenses shortens it. This conversion establishes a direct link between outflows and decision conditions. As time horizons shrink, decisions must be made more quickly, often under less favorable conditions.

Forced decisions arise when the system reaches points where action is required to maintain continuity. These points are defined by obligations that must be fulfilled regardless of conditions. High expense structures create recurring decision deadlines, as each obligation represents a moment at which the system must allocate resources. These deadlines are not optional. They are embedded within the system's structure, dictating the timing of decisions.

As expense pressure increases, the system's decision timing becomes externally dictated by these obligations. The system cannot delay or sequence decisions according to its own evaluation processes. It must act when required, even if conditions are unfavorable or information is incomplete. This reduces the system's control over its own decision-making process, as timing is no longer determined internally.

Expenses therefore create recurring points of forced action. Each obligation represents a moment at which the system must respond, regardless of its broader trajectory. The frequency of these moments is determined by the expense structure. Higher expenses increase the frequency of forced decisions, while lower expenses reduce it. This frequency directly influences the system's ability to operate deliberately rather than reactively.

Reducing expense pressure increases decision flexibility by extending the time between these forced action points. When obligations are lower, the system has greater freedom to determine when to act. This flexibility allows decisions to be aligned with conditions rather than with fixed deadlines. The system can evaluate alternatives, integrate information, and sequence actions more effectively.

Within the total expense structure, not all outflows contribute equally to system function. Leakage can be defined as outflows that do not materially support the system's operation or stability. These outflows persist within the system but do not enhance its capacity or improve its alignment. They represent a consumption of resources without a corresponding contribution to function.

Leakage increases total expense pressure without increasing system capability,directly competing with functional outflows for the same capacity. It accelerates the rate at which capacity is depleted while providing no structural benefit. This inefficiency reduces the system's ability to sustain operation and increases its proximity to constraint thresholds. The presence of leakage therefore weakens the system's overall efficiency.

Removing leakage improves system efficiency without altering its core structure. The system retains its functional capacity while reducing the rate at which resources are consumed. This adjustment lowers expense pressure, extending the system's time horizon and improving its ability to respond to variability. The reduction of leakage does not require fundamental changes to the system's design. It refines the alignment between outflows and function.

Expenses also perform a constraint enforcement function within the system. They act as continuous limitations on behavior by defining the obligations that must be maintained. These obligations shape the range of feasible actions available to the system. Higher expense structures impose tighter constraints, as a larger portion of capacity is committed to fulfilling obligations.

This constraint is active rather than passive. Expenses continuously restrict the system's ability to allocate resources to new or alternative pathways. They define what must be preserved, limiting the system's flexibility. As expense levels increase, the system's feasible decision space contracts. Fewer options remain available, as more capacity is dedicated to existing obligations.

Lower expense structures expand this feasible decision space by reducing the portion of capacity that is pre-committed. The system gains the ability to allocate resources more freely, exploring a wider range of potential actions. This expansion improves alignment by allowing decisions to be evaluated against a broader set of possibilities. Expense control therefore influences not only the level of pressure, but also the scope of available decisions.

The interaction between expense structure and other system mechanisms reinforces its central role. Within the Liquidity Buffer Mechanism, expenses determine the duration of runway by defining the rate at which liquidity is consumed. Higher expenses shorten this duration, while lower expenses extend it. The system's available time is therefore directly linked to its outflow structure.

Within the Scarcity Pressure Mechanism, high expenses accelerate the onset of scarcity by increasing the rate at which capacity is depleted. This acceleration forces decisions to be made under constrained conditions. Conversely, lower expenses delay the onset of scarcity, allowing the system to operate with reduced pressure.

Within the Margin Stability Mechanism, expense control influences the system's margin by determining how much capacity remains after obligations are met. Lower expenses increase this margin, providing a buffer against variability. Higher expenses reduce it, increasing the system's sensitivity to deviation.

Within the Constraint-Based Decision Mechanism, expenses define the structural limits within which decisions must operate. They establish the boundaries of feasible action, shaping the system's decision space. Within the Default Path Mechanism, expenses persist automatically unless actively changed, reinforcing the system's existing trajectory. These interactions demonstrate that expense structure is a central driver of system pressure across multiple dimensions.

At the system level, expense control influences decision quality indirectly by shaping the environment in which decisions are made. It does not alter the logic of decision-making itself. Instead, it modifies the conditions under which evaluation occurs. Reduced expense pressure extends decision timelines, providing more time for analysis and comparison.

Extended timelines allow for deeper evaluation, as the system can integrate more information and consider a wider range of alternatives. This depth improves alignment between decisions and system objectives. The improvement does not arise from changes in decision logic, but from the reduction of constraints that would otherwise limit evaluation.

Decision quality is therefore environment-dependent. The same system may produce different outcomes depending on the level of expense pressure it experiences. High-pressure environments compress evaluation, reduce optionality, and increase the frequency of forced decisions. Lower-pressure environments expand evaluation windows, increase flexibility, and allow for more deliberate sequencing.

Systems with controlled expenses operate with reduced urgency because they are further from constraint thresholds. This distance allows decisions to be made under less constrained conditions, improving alignment across time. The system maintains flexibility, as it is not required to respond immediately to recurring obligations.

Control of outflows reduces the frequency of forced decisions by extending the time between obligation-driven actions. This extension allows the system to operate with greater coherence, aligning decisions with conditions rather than with fixed deadlines. The system transitions from a reactive state, where actions are dictated by constraint, to a more controlled state, where decisions are formed within a broader temporal and structural context.

The system transitions from reacting to obligations to operating within controlled conditions.

The Risk Containment Mechanism

The Risk Containment Mechanism describes how a system limits the magnitude of adverse outcomes so that negative events do not translate into disproportionate reductions in capacity. Risk, in structural terms, is not the occurrence of an event but the exposure of the system to the consequences of that event. The distinction between occurrence and impact is central. Events may arise with varying frequency, but their significance is determined by how strongly they affect the system's ability to continue operating. Risk containment focuses on constraining this effect. It does not require predicting which events will occur. It requires defining how much damage any single event can inflict relative to the system's capacity. Exposure therefore determines how outcomes are translated into disruption. When exposure is high, even moderate events can produce large system effects. When exposure is bounded, even adverse outcomes remain within tolerable limits.

Downside represents negative deviation that reduces available capacity and shifts the system closer to constraint thresholds. The asymmetry between positive and negative outcomes defines how this deviation affects system stability. Gains increase capacity, but their effect is gradual and often distributed across time. Losses, by contrast, reduce capacity immediately, compressing the system's margin and altering its operating conditions. This asymmetry means that the structural significance of outcomes is not balanced. A reduction in capacity has a direct effect on decision conditions, while an equivalent increase does not necessarily restore those conditions at the same rate. Large losses alter the system's structure by reducing the buffer that absorbs variability and by increasing the pressure under which subsequent decisions must be made. As capacity declines, the system's tolerance for additional deviation diminishes. Downside control therefore functions as the primary stabilizing force by preserving capacity. Systems degrade through the accumulation of losses rather than through the absence of gains. Stability is maintained not by maximizing positive outcomes, but by limiting the scale of negative deviation that can occur.

Exposure defines the degree to which the system is affected by any given outcome. It acts as a scaling factor that translates external variability into internal impact. Two systems facing identical external conditions may experience different outcomes depending on their exposure levels. This difference arises not from the environment, but from how the system is structured relative to that environment. Exposure boundaries establish limits on this translation. They define the maximum effect that any single event can have on the system's state. By setting these limits, the system constrains the range of possible deviations from its baseline. Without such boundaries, the system remains fully coupled to external outcomes, allowing variability to pass through without restriction. With boundaries in place, adverse events are capped in their ability to influence the system. The presence of these limits ensures that variability does not directly scale into instability. Exposure boundaries therefore function as structural controls that define how far outcomes can deviate before they are contained.

Loss containment operates by restricting negative outcomes within predefined limits so that their effects do not propagate beyond their initial point of impact. Losses may either remain localized or extend across multiple components of the system. Containment interrupts the pathways through which losses spread. When containment is effective, the impact of a loss is confined to a specific segment, leaving the broader system intact. When containment is absent, the same loss can affect interconnected components, altering multiple decision pathways simultaneously. This difference defines the boundary between isolated deviation and systemic disruption. Contained losses preserve structural integrity by preventing cascading effects. The system absorbs the deviation within a limited area, maintaining continuity in its overall operation. Uncontained losses, by contrast, propagate through dependencies, amplifying their impact and increasing the likelihood of structural breakdown. The Risk Containment Mechanism therefore ensures that adverse outcomes remain bounded, preserving the coherence of the system under stress.

The interaction between risk containment, margin, and liquidity determines whether a system can absorb adverse outcomes without losing stability. Margin represents the capacity available beyond immediate obligations, providing a buffer that absorbs deviation. Liquidity represents the time available for the system to respond to changes in its state. Risk containment reduces the magnitude of losses entering the system, while margin determines whether those losses can be absorbed, and liquidity determines whether the system has sufficient time to respond. These elements function together. A contained loss that remains within the system's margin can be absorbed without altering its trajectory. Liquidity then provides the time required to adjust to the new state, restoring alignment if necessary. Without containment, losses may exceed margin, forcing immediate structural changes. Without liquidity, even contained losses may require rapid adjustment, reducing decision quality. The combination of containment and absorption defines resilience, allowing the system to sustain operation despite variability.

The structure of inflows and outflows influences how effectively losses can be managed once they occur. Expenses determine the rate at which capacity is consumed, while income determines the rate at which capacity is replenished. High expense structures increase the system's sensitivity to loss by accelerating capacity depletion. When exposure is also high, losses reduce capacity more quickly, bringing the system closer to constraint thresholds. In such configurations, even contained losses can produce rapid destabilization because the system lacks the margin to absorb them. Stable inflows, by contrast, provide a predictable source of replenishment, allowing the system to recover from contained losses more effectively. When expenses are controlled and income is stable, the system can restore capacity after a loss without requiring significant structural change. Risk containment interacts with these inflow and outflow dynamics by limiting the size of losses, but the system's ability to recover depends on how quickly capacity can be rebuilt and how slowly it is consumed. The balance between these elements determines whether containment leads to recovery or whether losses accumulate into instability.

Risk influences decision conditions before any adverse outcome is realized. Exposure exists as a structural property of the system, shaping its behavior in anticipation of potential loss. When exposure is high, the system becomes more sensitive to variability, as any deviation has the potential to produce significant impact. This sensitivity alters the conditions under which decisions are made. The system must account for the possibility of large losses, reducing its flexibility and narrowing its feasible decision space. Even in the absence of realized outcomes, exposure imposes constraints on behavior. Decisions are formed within the context of potential consequences, not only actual ones. When exposure is bounded, these constraints are reduced. The system operates with greater flexibility because the potential impact of adverse events is limited. Risk is therefore embedded within the system's structure, influencing decision-making independently of whether negative outcomes occur.

Error amplification describes the process through which small deviations expand into large system-level consequences. This expansion occurs when the system allows local misalignments to propagate through interconnected pathways. Exposure determines whether such propagation is possible. When exposure is high, even minor errors can scale into significant disruptions. When exposure is contained, errors remain localized, limiting their impact. The Risk Containment Mechanism reduces the pathways through which errors can amplify. By capping the potential impact of deviations, it ensures that small misalignments do not translate into large-scale instability. This function is closely linked to feedback delay and drift. When feedback is delayed, errors may persist without correction, increasing the risk of amplification. When drift accumulates, the system's trajectory diverges gradually, increasing the sensitivity to additional deviations. Containment limits the scale of these effects, stabilizing the system's long-term trajectory by preventing the escalation of error.

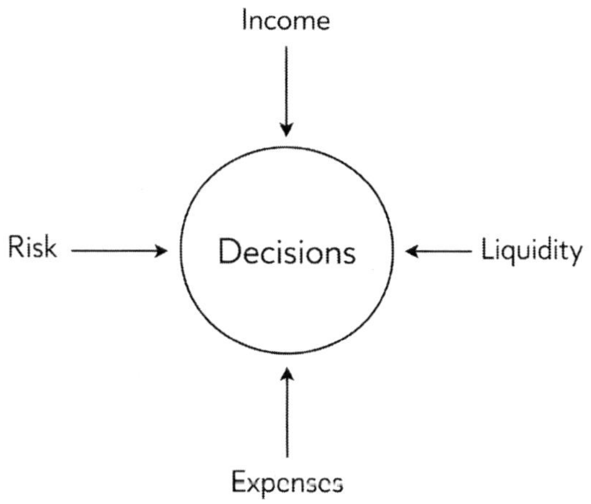

[Figure 5: System Interaction Map (Income–Liquidity–Expenses–Risk → Decisions)]

The system interaction map represents the structural relationship between the primary forces that shape decision conditions. At the center is the decision engine, which produces actions that influence the system's trajectory. Four directional flows converge on this engine. Income enters as a stabilizing input, providing predictability in resource inflows. Liquidity enters as a temporal input, extending the time available for evaluation and response. Expenses act as an output pressure, consuming capacity and compressing decision timelines. Risk enters as an exposure modifier, scaling the consequences of decisions and external variability. These forces interact continuously. Income stabilizes the input layer, reducing variability in available resources. Liquidity extends decision time, allowing for deeper evaluation. Expenses compress decision time by increasing the rate of capacity consumption. Risk modifies how decisions translate into outcomes by determining the scale of potential impact. Decisions therefore emerge from the combined influence of these forces. When the system is balanced, decision conditions remain stable, allowing for consistent alignment. When the system is imbalanced, one or more forces dominate, distorting decision conditions and increasing the likelihood of misalignment.

The interaction between these elements defines the system's ability to maintain stability under uncertainty. Balanced systems operate with predictable inputs, sufficient time, controlled outflows, and bounded exposure. In such configurations, variability does not translate directly into instability because the system can absorb and respond to it. Imbalanced systems exhibit the opposite characteristics. Unstable inputs increase uncertainty, limited liquidity compresses decision time, high expenses accelerate capacity depletion, and unbounded exposure amplifies the impact of adverse events. These conditions combine to create environments in which decisions are constrained and errors are more likely to propagate. The Risk Containment Mechanism operates within this broader structure by limiting how strongly adverse outcomes influence the system, but its effectiveness depends on the interaction with the other components.

Systems are not destabilized by uncertainty alone. Variability is inherent to any environment in which decisions are made. Instability arises when exposure to that variability is uncontained. When adverse outcomes can affect large portions of the system, even moderate variability can produce significant disruption. Limiting downside exposure preserves capacity by ensuring that losses remain within manageable bounds. This preservation allows the system to continue operating without crossing critical thresholds. By maintaining capacity, the system retains the ability to respond to future conditions, sustaining its decision-making function over time.

The Risk Containment Mechanism establishes that stability depends on controlling how much of the system is exposed to any single outcome. Variability cannot be eliminated, and outcomes cannot be predicted with complete accuracy. What can be structured is the extent to which those outcomes influence the system. By limiting downside magnitude, the system reduces the risk of capacity loss, stabilizes decision conditions, and prevents the amplification of error. Stability is therefore not achieved by removing uncertainty, but by ensuring that uncertainty does not translate into disproportionate disruption.

Control as Error Reduction

Control is commonly interpreted as the ability to make correct decisions consistently. This interpretation assumes that outcomes can be predicted with sufficient accuracy and that decisions can be evaluated against known future states. Under this view, control is equated with precision, where the system operates by selecting the optimal path at each decision point. The implication is that stability emerges from a sequence of correct choices, each reinforcing the intended trajectory. This framing depends on conditions that rarely exist in real-world systems.

Financial systems operate under uncertainty, constraint, and incomplete information. Decisions are formed without full visibility into future conditions, and the relationship between action and outcome is often indirect. Time pressure limits evaluation depth, variability alters inputs, and feedback is delayed. Under these conditions, the assumption of consistent correctness is structurally incompatible with how decisions are produced. Even when decisions are well-formed relative to available information, outcomes may diverge due to factors beyond the system's control.

Error, in this context, is not an exception but a continuous output. Decisions are made within environments that ensure variability in results. Accuracy fluctuates depending on timing, information availability, and external conditions. A system cannot rely on correctness as a stable foundation because correctness itself is variable and context-dependent.

The same decision structure may produce aligned outcomes in one environment and misalignment in another.

Control must therefore be defined independently of correctness. If stability depends on making correct decisions, then any deviation from accuracy introduces instability. Given that deviation is unavoidable, this definition leads to a system that is inherently fragile. A system that requires correctness to maintain alignment cannot sustain operation under real-world conditions. Control must instead be based on properties that remain stable even when decisions are imperfect.

Error emerges structurally from the interaction of multiple factors within the system. Inputs vary in both magnitude and timing, introducing uncertainty into resource availability. Feedback from decisions arrives after delays, often after subsequent decisions have already been made. Multiple variables interact simultaneously, producing outcomes that cannot be fully isolated to a single cause. Information is incomplete at the point of decision, requiring assumptions that may not align with actual conditions. These factors ensure that misalignment between expected and realized outcomes will occur.

Error can be defined as the deviation between the expected system state, as implied by decisions, and the realized system state after outcomes materialize. This deviation is not a failure condition. It is a normal byproduct of operating within an environment where uncertainty and variability are present. The system continuously produces outcomes that differ from expectations, not because of isolated mistakes, but because of structural limitations in prediction and evaluation.

The presence of error does not indicate that the system is malfunctioning. It indicates that the system is operating within its natural constraints. Variability ensures that outcomes will not perfectly match projections. Feedback delay ensures that corrections are not immediate. Multi-variable interaction ensures that cause and effect are not linear. These conditions make error unavoidable. Eliminating error would require eliminating uncertainty, which is not feasible within dynamic environments.

The relevant question is not whether error occurs, but how the system responds to it. A system that treats error as an exception will attempt to eliminate it through increased precision, which is structurally limited. A system that treats error as a constant will focus on managing its effects. This distinction defines the transition from correctness-based control to survivability-based control.

Control, in structural terms, can be defined as the ability of the system to continue operating despite the presence of error. This definition shifts the focus from the accuracy of individual decisions to the system's capacity to absorb deviation without losing alignment. Survivability under error becomes the defining characteristic of control. The system does not require perfect decisions to maintain stability. It requires the ability to withstand imperfect outcomes.

This capacity is composed of several interdependent elements. Tolerance represents the system's ability to absorb deviation without crossing failure thresholds. It is defined by the presence of buffers and overcapacity that separate normal operation from constraint. When tolerance is sufficient, errors can occur without forcing immediate structural change. The system remains within its operational range despite deviation.

Containment limits the extent to which errors propagate through the system. By bounding exposure, the system prevents local misalignments from scaling into systemic disruption. Containment ensures that adverse outcomes remain within defined limits, preserving the integrity of the overall structure. Without containment, even small errors can expand through interconnected pathways, amplifying their impact.

Time, as provided by liquidity, determines how long the system can operate before constraint forces action. Extended time horizons allow the system to respond to error under less compressed conditions. Liquidity creates the temporal space required for evaluation and correction. Without time, even contained errors may require immediate response, reducing decision quality.

The stability of inputs and outputs shapes the environment in which decisions are made. Stable income reduces variability in inflows, providing a consistent baseline for evaluation. Controlled expenses reduce the rate at which capacity is consumed, lowering the frequency of forced decisions. Together, these elements reduce pressure, allowing the system to operate with greater coherence.

Decision structure further stabilizes outcomes by reducing variability in how decisions are produced. Constraints, simplification, frameworks, and pre-commitment organize the decision process, limiting the range of possible errors. These structures do not eliminate error, but they reduce its frequency and magnitude by narrowing the decision space.

Control emerges from the interaction of these elements. It does not eliminate error, but it limits its impact and prevents propagation. A controlled system remains within its tolerance range despite continuous deviation. It absorbs, contains, and responds to error without crossing into instability.

Outcomes within a financial system are not determined solely by individual decisions. Decisions are produced within environments defined by system structure. These environments determine how decisions are formed, how they are evaluated, and how they translate into outcomes. The system shapes the conditions under which decisions occur, and those conditions influence the results.

Time pressure alters evaluation by compressing decision windows, reducing the depth of analysis. Complexity increases error probability by expanding the number of variables and interactions that must be processed. Lack of constraints expands the decision space, increasing the range of possible misalignments. Lack of margin amplifies consequences by reducing the system's ability to absorb deviation. Each of these factors is structural, not behavioral. They define the environment in which decisions are made.

The same decision can produce different outcomes depending on the system in which it occurs. In a system with sufficient margin and liquidity, a misaligned decision may be absorbed without significant impact. In a constrained system, the same decision may trigger a sequence of forced actions, leading to instability. This difference arises from system configuration rather than decision quality.

Decisions are therefore expressions of the system. They reflect the constraints, capacities, and structures within which they are formed. The system determines what decisions are possible, how they are evaluated, and how their outcomes affect the overall trajectory. Improving outcomes requires altering these underlying conditions rather than focusing exclusively on individual decisions.

Two approaches to managing financial systems can be contrasted. Decision optimization focuses on selecting the correct action in each instance. It assumes that control is achieved through precision and that improved outcomes result from better choices. This approach relies on the ability to predict outcomes and to evaluate decisions accurately in real time.

System design, by contrast, focuses on structuring the conditions under which decisions are made. It recognizes that variability and uncertainty limit the effectiveness of optimization. Instead of attempting to achieve correctness in each instance, it creates environments in which decisions are more likely to remain within acceptable bounds. Design determines the system's capacity for time, exposure, variability, and error tolerance.

Optimization is sensitive to changes in conditions. Under pressure or uncertainty, the ability to select the correct decision diminishes. Design remains stable across varying conditions because it shapes the environment itself. A well-structured system produces more consistent outcomes even when individual decisions are imperfect.

The system determines the time available for decision-making, the level of exposure to adverse outcomes, the variability in inputs, and the tolerance for error. These factors influence decision quality more directly than the attempt to optimize individual choices. Better systems produce better average outcomes by reducing the conditions that lead to misalignment.

Stability emerges from structure rather than from isolated correctness. It is the result of a system that can absorb variability, contain error, and maintain alignment across time. Individual decisions contribute to outcomes, but their impact is mediated by the system in which they occur.

Stability is not a fixed state. It is a dynamic condition maintained through continuous interaction between system components. Drift causes gradual misalignment as small deviations accumulate over time. Feedback delay slows the system's ability to detect and correct these deviations. External conditions change, altering the environment in which the system operates.

Maintaining stability requires ongoing recalibration. The system must adjust its structure in response to changes in conditions and to the accumulation of error. Liquidity enables this process by providing the time necessary for correction. Constraints limit the range of possible errors, reducing the scale of misalignment. Frameworks stabilize decision processes, ensuring consistency across cycles. Default pathways execute the system's structure continuously, reinforcing its configuration. Risk containment limits the damage from adverse outcomes, preserving capacity.

These mechanisms interact to maintain alignment. Stability is not achieved through a single decision or adjustment, but through the continuous operation of the system within its tolerance range. As conditions change and errors accumulate, the system must adapt to remain within that range.

A stable financial system does not depend on correct decisions. It does not eliminate uncertainty, nor does it avoid variability. Instead, it absorbs error, limits exposure, extends time, reduces forced decisions, and operates through structured processes. These properties allow the system to maintain continuity despite the presence of misalignment.

Control is not precision. It is the ability to contain the effects of deviation so that they do not compromise the system's operation. Control is tolerance, defined by the capacity to absorb error without crossing failure thresholds. Control is time, provided by liquidity, allowing the system to respond before constraints force action. These elements define the system's ability to remain intact under imperfect conditions.

Stability is not achieved by making perfect decisions, but by operating within a system that remains intact when decisions are imperfect.

The Money Stability Series

Money Stability: *How to Build Financial Control in an Unstable World* (Cornerstone Volume)

Liquidity and Runway: *How to Build Financial Time, Extend Your Runway, and Stay Stable in an Unstable Economy*

Income Stability: *How to Build Predictable, Durable, and Resilient Income*

Expense Stability: *How to Control Spending, Reduce Leakage, and Create Consistency*

Risk Stability: *How to Control Exposure, Limit Downside, and Stay Financially Stable*

Financial Decisions: *How to Reduce Mistakes, Limit Risk, and Make Better Decisions Under Uncertainty*

Future titles expand the Money Stability framework:

Governance Stability

Financial Stability

Part of a Broader Stability Framework

The Money Stability Series is part of a larger stability ecosystem published by Perennial Publishing.

Related domains include:

Metabolic Stability — biological load, energy, and recovery capacity

Career Stability — income durability, positioning, and transition resilience

Mental Stability — cognitive steadiness under pressure and uncertainty

Emotional Stability — regulatory steadiness in environments that do not slow down

Each domain approaches stability as a structural problem: capacity versus load, buffers versus shocks, and governance versus drift. Together, they form a unified framework for long-horizon durability across the major systems that determine life trajectory.

About Perennial Publishing

Perennial Publishing produces practical systems guides for building stability in an unstable world.

Our books explore the foundations of long-term resilience across health, finance, career, and everyday decision-making. Each title focuses on clear frameworks, durable principles, and practical strategies that help readers build lasting stability rather than short-term fixes.

The Perennial catalog includes series on metabolic health, financial stability, career systems, and personal consistency. While each book stands on its own, they share a common goal: helping individuals create durable systems that support a stable and sustainable life.

Made in United States
North Haven, CT
04 November 2026

21765026R00113